D0586638

Lawyer's
Wit and Wisdom

Quotations on the Legal Profession
In brief.

Compiled by
Kathryn Zullo

Copyright © 1995, 2001 by Nash & Zullo Productions, Inc.
Copyright © 2010 by The Wordsellers, Inc.
All rights reserved.

The right of Kathryn Zullo to be identified as the author has been asserted in accordance with the Copyright, Design and Patents Act 1988.

Published in Great Britain in 2010 by Carbolic Smoke Ball Co.

Carbolic Smoke Ball Co.
Silverbeck
Jumps Road
Churt
Farnham
GU10 2HL

Tel. +44 (0)1252 795951
www.carbolicsmokeball.com

All rights reserved; no part of this publication may be reproduced, stored in a retrieval system, or transmitted in any form or by any means, electronic, mechanical, photocopying, recording, or otherwise without the prior written consent of the Publisher. This book may not be lent, resold, hired out or otherwise disposed of by way of trade in any form of binding or cover other than that in which it is published without the prior written consent of the Publisher.

British Library Cataloguing in Publication Data
A CIP record for this book can be obtained from the British Library.

ISBN 978-0-9556557-2-2

Printed and bound by the MPG Books Group, Bodmin and Kings Lynn

Dedication

To my son-in-law Danny Manausa, whose legal
wisdom is matched only by his clever wit.

KATHRYN ZULLO

Contents

Acknowledgements   vi

Introduction   vii

The People

    The Law   1
    Lawyers   15
    Clients   29
    Law Firms   37
    Judges   41
    Juries   51
    Witnesses   57
    The Supreme Court   63

Codes of Conduct

    Ethics   69
    Government   75
    Law School   79
    Obeying the Law   83
    Justice   89
    Injustice   101

The Wheels of Justice

    Litigation   107
    The Trial   113
    The Verdict   119

Closing Arguments

    The Profession   125
    Legal Fees   133
    Courtroom Performance   139
    The System   145
    On Reform   155
    Advice to Lawyers   161

Index   167

Acknowledgements

I wish to thank the American Bar Association for its cooperation in allowing me to adapt many of the anecdotes in this book from two of its publications.

Several anecdotes were first reported in the monthly "Worst Stories" feature in the *ABA Journal*, which graciously granted me permission to edit and reprint them.

Other anecdotes were adapted from an annual feature called "Legal Lunacies" by Barbara Kate Repa, which appeared in *Student Lawyer* magazine, also published by the ABA. *Student Lawyer* granted me permission to edit and reprint these items, for which I am grateful.

Finally, I wish to thank *Reader's Digest* for allowing me to reprint five anecdotes that had originally appeared in earlier issues.

Introduction

No group is exalted or vilified more than lawyers. In Shakespeare's Henry VI, Dick the Butcher fantasizes: "The first thing we do, let's kill all the lawyers." That's probably the world's favorite quote regarding the profession. But before Dick's sympathizers judge too quickly, they should at least weigh the testimony of the late defense attorney Ellis Rubin: "Being a lawyer is about serving justice. That's not only our greatest calling, it's our only calling."

The legal profession triggers diverse opinions and feelings because lawyers deal with extremes of the human condition, usually interacting with people in times of great need and stress. As famed jurist Oliver Wendell Holmes Jr. once said, "In what other [profession] does one plunge so deep in the stream of life, so share its passions, its battles, its despair, its triumphs, both as witness and actor?"

Although the law has changed over the centuries, the relationship between attorneys and clients has remained pretty much the same. It's still a love-hate affair. No wonder people from all walks of life have never been at a loss for words when revealing their true feelings about lawyers. In this book, quotations range from the insightful and pithy statements from famous judges and philosophers to light-hearted quips from fictional characters and satirists. And sometimes truth is stranger than fiction, as the leavening of humorous true-life anecdotes about life in the legal world.

Words have been – and always will be – the basic tools of the lawyer. Said noted legal scholar Charles Alan Wright, "Whether we are trying a case, writing a brief, drafting a contract, or negotiating with an adversary, words are the only things we have to work with."

THE PEOPLE

THE PEOPLE

THE LAW

Common sense often makes a good law.
WILLIAM O. DOUGLAS,
SUPREME COURT JUSTICE

If you like laws and sausages, you should never watch either
one being made.
OTTO VON BISMARCK,
19TH-CENTURY PRUSSIAN PRINCE

The citizen is the law. In this country we haven't got around
to understanding that. We think of the law as an enemy.
DISTRICT ATTORNEY SEWELL ENDICOTT,
IN THE 1949 NOVEL *THE LITTLE SISTER* BY RAYMOND CHANDLER

It is a besetting vice of democracies to substitute public
opinion for law. This is the usual form in which masses of
men exhibit their tyranny.
JAMES FENIMORE COOPER,
IN HIS 1838 POLITICAL ESSAY *THE AMERICAN DEMOCRAT*

The law is not a machine and the judges not machine-
tenders. There never was and there never will be a body of
fixed and predetermined rules alike for all.
JEROME N. FRANK,
AMERICAN JUDGE

From Watergate we learned what generations before us have known – our Constitution works. And during Watergate years it was interpreted again so as to reaffirm that no one – absolutely no one – is above the law.

LEON JAWORSKI,
SPECIAL PROSECUTOR FOR THE WATERGATE TRIALS

Without the law, there can be no justice. And without justice, there can be no freedom.

SAM WATERSTON,
AS JACK MCCOY, DISTRICT ATTORNEY IN THE TELEVISION SHOW *LAW AND ORDER*

No law or ordinance is mightier than understanding.

PLATO, 1ST-CENTURY GREEK PHILOSOPHER

To be effective, a law must have the support of the majority of the people it impacts. To get that support, a law must be enforceable, fairly applied, understood and consistent with society's values.

THOMAS A. WARTOWSKI, AMERICAN LAWYER

I decided the law was the exact opposite of sex; even when it was good it was lousy.

MORTIMER ZUCKERMAN,
AMERICAN EDITOR AND PUBLISHER

The law is like the killy-loo bird, a creature that insisted on flying backward because it didn't care where it was going but was mightily interested where it had been.

FRED RODELL, YALE LAW PROFESSOR

The laws sometimes sleep, but never die.

ANONYMOUS

All laws are an attempt to domesticate the natural ferocity
of the species.

JOHN W. GARDNER,
U.S. SECRETARY HEALTH, EDUCATION AND WELFARE

Law is born from despair of human nature.

JOSÉ ORTEGA Y GASSET,
19TH-CENTURY SPANISH PHILOSOPHER

The law, in its majestic equality, forbids all men to sleep
under bridges, to beg in the streets, and to steal bread – the
rich as well as the poor.

ANATOLE FRANCE,
19TH-CENTURY FRENCH WRITER

The wording of laws should mean the same thing to all
men.

CHARLES LOUIS DE MONTESQUIEU,
18TH-CENTURY FRENCH LAWYER AND POLITICAL PHILOSOPHER

Laws are felt only when the individual comes into conflict
with them.

SUZANNE LA FOLLETTE,
AMERICAN POLITICIAN AND FEMINIST

Where-ever Law ends, Tyranny begins.

JOHN LOCKE,
17TH-CENTURY ENGLISH PHILOSOPHER

Law is a pledge that the citizens of a state will do justice to
one another.

LYCOPHRON,
3RD-CENTURY B.C. GREEK POET AND SCHOLAR

The law: It has honored us; may we honor it.

DANIEL WEBSTER,
18TH-CENTURY AMERICAN STATESMAN, ORATOR AND LAWYER

If we desire respect for the law we must first make the law respectable.

LOUIS D. BRANDEIS,
SUPREME COURT JUSTICE

Good laws lead to the making of better ones; bad ones bring about worse.

JEAN JACQUES ROUSSEAU,
18TH-CENTURY FRENCH PHILOSOPHER AND WRITER

Riches without law are more dangerous than is poverty without law.

HENRY WARD BEECHER,
19TH-CENTURY AMERICAN CLERGYMAN

I say that you cannot administer a wicked law impartially. You can only destroy. You can only punish. I warn you that a wicked law, like cholera, destroys everyone it touches – its upholders as well as its defiers.

SPENCER TRACY AS HENRY DRUMMOND
IN THE 1960 FILM *INHERIT THE WIND*

Nothing is more destructive of respect for the government and the law of the land than passing laws which cannot be enforced.

ALBERT EINSTEIN,
GERMAN-BORN AMERICAN PHYSICIST

Possession isn't nine-tenths of the law. It's nine-tenths of the problem.

JOHN LENNON, MUSICIAN, POET, WRITER AND PEACE ACTIVIST

It may be true that the law cannot make a man love me, but it can keep him from lynching me, and I think that's pretty important.

DR. MARTIN LUTHER KING JR.,
AMERICAN CLERGYMAN AND CIVIL RIGHTS LEADER

Whereas the law is passionless, passion must never sway the heart of man.

ARISTOTLE,
4TH-CENTURY B.C. GREEK PHILOSOPHER

Law is a Bottomless-Pit, it is a Cormorant, a Harpy, that devours every thing.

JOHN ARBUTHNOT,
17TH-CENTURY SCOTTISH PHYSICIAN AND WRITER

Law: an ordinance of reason for the common good, made by him who has care of the community.

ST. THOMAS AQUINAS,
13TH-CENTURY ITALIAN THEOLOGIAN

The good of the people is the supreme law.

CICERO,
2ND-CENTURY B.C. ROMAN STATESMAN, ORATOR AND WRITER

Law is a formless mass of isolated decisions.

MORRIS COHEN,
RUSSIAN-BORN AMERICAN PHILOSOPHER

Laws should be like clothes. They should be made to fit the people they are meant to serve.

CLARENCE DARROW,
AMERICAN LAWYER AND AUTHOR

Law is order, and good law is good order.

ARISTOTLE,
4TH-CENTURY B.C. GREEK PHILOSOPHER

The law is a sort of hocus-pocus science that smiles in yer face while it picks yer pocket.

CHARLES MACKLIN,
18TH-CENTURY IRISH ACTOR AND DRAMATIST

Law and order are always and everywhere the law and order which protect the established hierarchy.

HERBERT MARCUSE,
GERMAN-BORN AMERICAN PHILOSOPHER

Men have feelings but the law does not.

NAPOLEON I,
EMPEROR OF FRANCE

Law is a majestic edifice, sheltering all of us, each stone of which rests on another.

JOHN GALSWORTHY,
19TH-CENTURY ENGLISH WRITER AND DRAMATIST

The law is the true embodiment of everything that's excellent.

WILLIAM S. GILBERT,
19TH-CENTURY ENGLISH POET AND WRITER

A law can be both economic folly and constitutional.

ANTONIN SCALIA,
SUPREME COURT JUSTICE

Law is the harmony of the world.

RICHARD HOOKER,
16TH-CENTURY ENGLISH THEOLOGIAN

The law is so phallic! It doesn't leave much room for sensitivity, which must be why so many guys are happy in it.

ALYSON SINGER,
AMERICAN LAWYER

Law is experience developed by reason and applied continually to further experience.

ROSCOE POUND,
DEAN EMERITUS, HARVARD LAW SCHOOL

The law is not majestic. The law is what public opinion says it is. I could tell you a lot about the law ...We got a man to argue for me tomorrow who wouldn't have me to dinner in his house. He talks on the phone with the president. But I have paid his price and he will be at my side for as long as it takes.

DUTCH SCHULTZ,
NOTORIOUS DEPRESSION-ERA MOBSTER,
IN THE 1989 NOVEL *BILLY BATHGATE* BY E. L. DOCTOROW

Law is the backbone which keeps man erect.

S. C. YUTER,
AMERICAN JOURNALIST AND WRITER

We know that the Law is good, if a man use it lawfully.

1 TIMOTHY 1:8

Law is but a heathen word for prayer.

DANIEL DEFOE,
17TH-CENTURY ENGLISH WRITER

The law is reason free from passion.

ARISTOTLE,
4TH-CENTURY B.C. GREEK PHILOSOPHER

The law will never make men free; it is men who have got to make the law free.

HENRY DAVID THOREAU,
19TH-CENTURY AMERICAN WRITER

The more laws, the more offenders.

THOMAS FULLER,
17TH-CENTURY ENGLISH WRITER

The laws of a nation form the most instructive portion of its history.

EDWARD GIBBON,
18TH-CENTURY ENGLISH HISTORIAN

Woman throughout the ages has been mistress to the law, as man has been its master.

FREDA ADLER,
AMERICAN EDUCATOR

The law sees and treats women the way men see and treat women.

CATHARINE MACKINNON,
AMERICAN LAW PROFESSOR, FEMINIST AND WRITER

It usually takes a hundred years to make a law, and then, after it has done its work, it usually takes a hundred years to get rid of it.

HENRY WARD BEECHER,
19TH-CENTURY AMERICAN CLERGYMAN

The law can never make us as secure as we are when we do not need it.

ALEXANDER M. BICKEL,
ROMANIAN-BORN AMERICAN LEGAL SCHOLAR

The criminal law represents the pathology of civilization.

MORRIS COHEN,
RUSSIAN-BORN AMERICAN PHILOSOPHER

Laws too gentle are seldom obeyed; too severe, seldom executed.

BENJAMIN FRANKLIN,
18TH-CENTURY AMERICAN STATESMAN AND PHILOSOPHER

I know no method to secure the repeal of bad or obnoxious laws so effective as their stringent execution.

ULYSSES S. GRANT,
18TH PRESIDENT OF THE UNITED STATES

A strict observance of the written laws is doubtless one of the high virtues of a good citizen, but it is not the highest. The laws of necessity, of self-preservation, of saving our country when in danger, are of higher obligation.

THOMAS JEFFERSON,
3RD PRESIDENT OF THE UNITED STATES

It is difficult to make our material condition better by the best laws, but it is easy enough to ruin it by bad laws.

THEODORE ROOSEVELT,
26TH PRESIDENT OF THE UNITED STATES

Many laws as certainly make bad men, as bad men make many laws.

WALTER SAVAGE LANDOR,
19TH-CENTURY ENGLISH WRITER

Moral principle is the foundation of law.

RONALD D. DWORKIN,
NEW YORK UNIVERSITY LAW PROFESSOR

A multitude of laws in a country is like a great number of
physicians, a sign of weakness and malady.

VOLTAIRE, 18TH-CENTURY FRENCH WRITER

The best law leaves the least discretion to the judge.

LATIN PROVERB

The laws put the safety of all above the safety of one.

CICERO,
2ND-CENTURY B.C. ROMAN STATESMAN, ORATOR AND WRITER

The purpose of law is to prevent the strong from always
having their way.

OVID,
1ST-CENTURY ROMAN POET

As physicians are the preservers of the sick, so are the laws
of the injured.

EPICTETUS,
2ND-CENTURY B.C. GREEK PHILOSOPHER

Every law which originated in ignorance and malice, and
gratifies the passions from which it sprang, we call the
wisdom of our ancestors.

SYDNEY SMITH,
19TH-CENTURY ENGLISH WRITER

Laws are inherited like diseases.

JOHANN WOLFGANG VON GOETHE,
18TH-CENTURY GERMAN POET AND DRAMATIST

No laws, however stringent, can make the idle industrious,
the thriftless provident, or the drunken sober.

SAMUEL SMILES, 19TH-CENTURY ENGLISH WRITER

Men would be great criminals did they need as many laws
as they make.

LORD C. J. DARLING,
19TH-CENTURY ENGLISH JUDGE

When men are pure, laws are useless; when men are
corrupt, laws are broken.

BENJAMIN DISRAELI, 19TH-CENTURY BRITISH PRIME MINISTER

Someone has tabulated that we have 35 million laws on the
books to enforce the Ten Commandments.

ATTRIBUTED TO BERT MASTERSON AND EARL WILSON,
AMERICAN JOURNALISTS

Laws are spider webs; they hold the weak and delicate who
are caught in their meshes, but are torn in pieces by the rich
and powerful.

ANACHARSIS, 6TH-CENTURY B.C. SCYTHIAN PHILOSOPHER

The law is a gun, which if it misses a pigeon always kills a
crow; if it does not strike the guilty, it hits someone else. As
every crime creates a law, so in turn every law creates a crime.

EDWARD GEORGE EARLE LYTTON BULWER-LYTTON,
ENGLISH NOVELIST AND POLITICIAN

Law is certain in meaning, just in precept, convenient in
execution, agreeable to the form of government, and
productive of virtue in those that live under it.

FRANCIS BACON,
17TH-CENTURY ENGLISH PHILOSOPHER AND WRITER

Laws are not made for a righteous man, but for the lawless
and disobedient, for the ungodly and for sinners.

1 TIMOTHY, 1:9

Postulating on the predominating principles of pollution

In his opinion in a case involving the dumping of garbage in an unauthorized area, Georgia Appellate Judge H. Sol Banks proved he was an avid alliterationist. He wrote:

"Preventing public pollution permits promiscuous perusal of personality but persistent perspicacious patron persuasively provided pertinent perdurable preponderating presumption precedent preventing prison."

In other words, the defendant was found not guilty.

When no means no

In a 1973 decision involving school segregation in Denver, Supreme Court Justice William J. Brennan Jr., achieved great notoriety among fellow jurists. It wasn't for his opinion, but for his penning of the Court's first quadruple negative sentence. He wrote:

"This is not to say, however, that the prima facie case may not be met by evidence supporting a finding that a lesser degree of segregated schooling in the core city area would not have resulted even if the Board had not acted as it did."

A great judge of weather

Samuel King, a U.S. District Court Judge in California, was annoyed that bad weather was keeping people from showing up for jury duty.

On February 18, 1986, he decreed: "I hereby order that it cease raining by Tuesday." California then suffered five years of drought.

So in 1991, he issued another decree: "I hereby rescind my

order of February 18, 1986, and order that rain shall fall in California beginning February 27, 1991."

Days later, the state was hit by its heaviest rains in ten years.

From here to eternity

A lease offered by a South Florida shopping center developer contains the following "End of the World" clause:

"If the end of the world is imminent before all Tenant's obligations are fully performed, then Landlord may elect to declare all rents to the end of the term to be immediately due and payable in full and may be enforced against Tenant by any available procedure. For remedial purposes, Landlord will be deemed aligned with the forces of light, and Tenant with forces of darkness, regardless of the parties' actual ultimate destinations, unless and until Landlord elects otherwise in writing."

LAWYERS

A lawyer's relationship to justice and wisdom ... is on a par with a piano tuner's relationship to a concert. He neither composes the music, nor interprets it – he merely keeps the machinery running.

LUCILLE KALLEN, TELEVISION COMEDY WRITER

Lawyers are ... operators of the toll bridge across which anyone in search of justice must pass.

JANE BRYANT QUINN, AMERICAN JOURNALIST

Being a lawyer is about serving justice. That's not only our greatest calling, it's our only calling.

ELLIS RUBIN, AMERICAN LAWYER

The lawyer's job in practice is to be on one hand the impassioned representative of his client to the world, and on the other the wise representative to his client of the legal system and the society, explaining and upholding the demands and restrictions that system places on them both.

SCOTT TUROW,
AMERICAN LAWYER AND NOVELIST

A personal injury lawyer is in a position to level the playing field and help people under our legal system.

PHILIP CORBOY,
AMERICAN LAWYER

15

To be an effective criminal defense counsel, an attorney must be prepared to be demanding, outrageous, irreverent, blasphemous, a rogue, a renegade, and a hated, isolated and lonely person ... Few love a spokesman for the despised and the damned.

CLARENCE DARROW,
AMERICAN LAWYER AND WRITER

Most good lawyers live well, work hard, and die poor.

DANIEL WEBSTER,
19TH-CENTURY AMERICAN STATESMAN, ORATOR AND LAWYER

The trial lawyer does what Socrates was executed for: making the worse argument appear the stronger.

IRVING R. KAUFMAN,
U.S. COURT OF APPEALS JUDGE

Law is a profession which abounds with honorable men, and in which there are fewer scamps than in any other.

GEORGE BORROW,
19TH-CENTURY ENGLISH WRITER AND LINGUIST

A good lawyer has a grasp of what yesterday teaches us about today and tomorrow, and knows that the real meaning of words like "freedom" or "justice" can only be found in the tapestry of history.

SOL M. LINOWITZ,
AMERICAN LAWYER

Anyone who believes a better day dawns when lawyers are eliminated bears the burden of explaining who will take their place. Who will protect the poor, the injured, the victims of negligence, the victims of racial discrimination and the victims of racial violence.

JOHN J. CURTIN JR., AMERICAN LAWYER

I've never met a litigator who didn't think he was winning –
right up until the moment the guillotine dropped.

WILLIAM F. BAXTER,
ASSISTANT U.S. ATTORNEY GENERAL

You cannot live without the lawyers, and certainly you
cannot die without them.

JOSEPH H. CHOATE,
AMERICAN LAWYER AND DIPLOMAT

A lawyer is a learned gentleman who rescues your estate
from your enemies and keeps it himself.

LORD HENRY PETER BROUGHAM,
19TH-CENTURY SCOTTISH JUDGE AND POLITICAL LEADER

I am not so afraid of lawyers as I used to be. They are lambs
in wolves' clothing.

EDNA ST. VINCENT MILLAY,
AMERICAN POET

The animals are not as stupid as one thinks – they have
neither doctors nor lawyers.

L. DOCQUIER,
FRENCH APHORIST

Lawyers are like rhinoceroses: thick skinned, short-sighted,
and always ready to charge.

DAVID MELLOR, BRITISH POLITICIAN

My daddy is a movie actor, and sometimes he plays the
good guy, and sometimes he plays the lawyer.

MALCOLM FORD,
ON WHAT HIS FATHER, ACTOR HARRISON FORD, DOES FOR A LIVING

Only painters and lawyers can change white to black.

JAPANESE PROVERB

Show me your briefs and I'll show you mine.

PLJ,
SEEKING "AN ATTRACTIVE, SLIM & WITTY SINGLE WHITE FEMALE LAWYER,
25-30, FOR 'COURT-SHIP,'" THROUGH 'PERSONALS FOR PROFESSIONALS'
IN *THE NEW YORK LAW JOURNAL*

Lawyers like to throw around jargon and flowery language because it makes them feel self-important and prestigious.

GEORGE HATHAWAY,
AMERICAN WRITER

I don't know of any other industry, except the movie business, that has so many stars. Every lawyer thinks he's special.

PETER MORRISON,
AMERICAN LAWYER

No splints yet invented will heal a lawyer's broken reputation.

PAUL O'NEIL,
AMERICAN JOURNALIST AND WRITER

You want the unvarnished and ungarnished truth, and I'm no hand for that. I'm a lawyer.

MCKNIGH
IN THE 1909 NOVEL *THE MAN IN LOWER TEN*
BY MARY ROBERTS RINEHART

The New England folks have a saying, that three Philadelphia lawyers are a match for the very devil himself.

SALEM OBSERVER

Lawyers take to politics like bears take to honey.

ROBERT TOWNSEND,
AMERICAN BUSINESSMAN

A peasant between two lawyers is like a fish between two cats.

SPANISH PROVERB

What chance has the ignorant, uncultivated liar against the educated expert? What chance have I ... against a lawyer?

MARK TWAIN,
AMERICAN WRITER AND HUMORIST

I have a high opinion of lawyers. With all their faults, they stack up well against those in every other occupation or profession. They are better to work with or play with or fight with or drink with than most other varieties of mankind.

HARRISON TWEED,
AMERICAN LAWYER

A lawyer with a briefcase can steal more than a hundred men with guns.

DON CORLEONE,
MARIO PUZO'S *THE GODFATHER*

I think we may class the lawyer in the natural history of monsters.

JOHN KEATS,
19TH-CENTURY ENGLISH POET

The best description of "utter waste" would be a busload of lawyers to go over a cliff with three empty seats.

LAMAR HUNT,
OWNER, KANSAS CITY CHIEFS FOOTBALL TEAM

A lawyer without history or literature is a mechanic, a mere working mason.

SIR WALTER SCOTT,
18TH-CENTURY SCOTTISH POET AND WRITER

Why is there always a secret singing when a lawyer cashes in? Why does a hearse horse snicker hauling a lawyer away?

CARL SANDBURG,
AMERICAN WRITER

Lawyer: The only man in whom ignorance of the law is not punished.

ELBERT HUBBARD,
19TH-CENTURY AMERICAN WRITER AND EDITOR

A lawyer's job is to manipulate the skeletons in other people's closets.

SOL STEIN,
AMERICAN BUSINESSMAN AND WRITER

The one great principle of English law is to make business for itself.

CHARLES DICKENS, 19TH-CENTURY ENGLISH WRITER

When God wanted to chastise mankind, He invented lawyers.

RUSSIAN PROVERB

Some people think that a lawyer's business is to make white black; but his real business is to make white in spite of the stained and soiled condition which renders its true color questionable. He is simply an intellectual washing machine.

LOGAN E. BLECKLEY,
AMERICAN JUDGE

A lawyer's dream of heaven – every man reclaimed his property at the resurrection, and each tried to recover it from all his forefathers.

SAMUEL BUTLER,
19TH-CENTURY ENGLISH JOURNALIST AND WRITER

When there's a rift in the lute, the business of the lawyer is to widen the rift and gather the loot.

ARTHUR HAYS,
AMERICAN LAWYER

Lawyers use the law as shoemakers use leather: rubbing it, pressing it, and stretching it with their teeth, all to the end of making it fit for their purposes.

LOUIS XII,
KING OF FRANCE

If you can think of something which is connected with something without thinking of the something it is connected to, you have a legal mind.

THOMAS REED POWELL,
HARVARD PROFESSOR

Lawyers are always more ready to get a man into troubles than out of them.

OLIVER GOLDSMITH,
18TH-CENTURY ENGLISH WRITER

God works wonders now and then: Behold: a lawyer, an honest man.

BENJAMIN FRANKLIN,
18TH-CENTURY AMERICAN STATESMAN AND PHILOSOPHER

Lawyer: One skilled in circumvention of the law.

AMBROSE BIERCE, AMERICAN WRITER

Young lawyers attend the courts, not because they have business there but because they have no business anywhere else.

WASHINGTON IRVING,
19TH-CENTURY AMERICAN WRITER

The Devil makes his Christmas pie of lawyers' tongues.

ENGLISH PROVERB

Of course the cameras make some lawyers grandstand, but that's the way some lawyers are anyway. They talk for a living.

NANCY GRACE,
AMERICAN LAWYER AND TV PERSONALITY

Mr. Attorney, I respect you, I fear you not; and the less you speak of your own greatness, the more I will think of it.
Francis Bacon, 17th-century English philosopher and writer
No lawyer will ever go to Heaven so long as there is room for more in Hell.

FRENCH PROVERB

I didn't become a lawyer because I like the law. The law sucks. It's boring, but it can be used as a weapon. You want to bankrupt somebody? Cost him everything he's worked for? Make his wife leave him, make his kids cry... yeah, we can do that.

RICHARD FISH,
SENIOR PARTNER IN THE TELEVISION SHOW *ALLY MCBEAL*

There are three sorts of lawyers – able, unable and lamentable.

ROBERT SMITH SURTEES,
19TH-CENTURY ENGLISH NOVELIST

Lawyers have been and remain in the forefront of the battles to guarantee equality and justice for all Americans, and to enforce the protection of the Bill of Rights and the civil rights laws.

CHARISSE LILLIE, CHAIR OF THE AMERICAN BAR ASSOCIATION COMMISSION ON OPPORTUNITIES FOR MINORITIES IN THE PROFESSION

The attitude of those of us who have anything to do with it [the law] should be that of the familiar sign in the western dance hall, "Don't shoot the piano player. He's doing the best he can."

WILLIAM PROSSER, LEGAL SCHOLAR

Lawyer: an individual whose principal role is to protect his clients from others of his profession.

ANONYMOUS

The minute you read something you don't understand, you can be almost sure it was drawn up by a lawyer.

WILL ROGERS, AMERICAN HUMORIST

Old lawyers never die, they just lose their appeal.

ANONYMOUS

Whatever their failings as a class may be, and however likely to lose their immortal souls, lawyers do not generally lose papers.

ARTHUR TRAIN,
AMERICAN LAWYER AND WRITER

Lawyers: persons who write a 10,000-word document and call it a brief.

FRANZ KAFKA, CZECHOSLOVAKIAN NOVELIST

It is a horrible demoralizing thing to be a lawyer. You look for such low motives in everyone and everything.

KATHERINE T. HINKSON,
IRISH POET AND WRITER

I happen to be dumb lucky because I grew up in a town where lawyers are people whom people look to for solutions. And who in their right mind, given that role, would not want to fulfill it?

DAVE SOUCY, AMERICAN LAWYER

Lawyers, like bread, [are best] when they are young and new.

THOMAS FULLER,
17TH-CENTURY ENGLISH CLERGYMAN AND WRITER

A man without money needs no more fear a crowd of lawyers than a crowd of pickpockets.

WILLIAM WYCHERLEY, 17TH-CENTURY ENGLISH WRITER

He saw a lawyer killing a viper.
On a dunghill hard by his own stable,
And the Devil smiled, for it put him in mind
Of Cain and his brother, Abel.

SAMUEL TAYLOR COLERIDGE,
18TH-CENTURY ENGLISH POET

A barrister of extended practice, if he has any talents at all, is the best companion in the world.

SIR WALTER SCOTT,
18TH-CENTURY SCOTTISH POET AND WRITER

Lawyers and soldiers are the Devil's playmates.

FRENCH PROVERB

The bar is still dominated by shortsightedness and self-interest. Spotting change there is like watching a glacier move.

VERNON COUNTRYMAN,
PROFESSOR, HARVARD UNIVERSITY

Most lawyers are like whores. They serve the client who puts the highest fee on the table.

FLORYNCE RAE KENNEDY,
AMERICAN LAWYER AND CIVIL RIGHTS ACTIVIST

A lot of defense attorneys take the facts of the case and twist them around and try, in effect, to create a lie out of some truth.

JOHN KATZENBACH,
AMERICAN JOURNALIST

Attorneys are just good followers ...The lawyer mentality is to follow the rules and make a big pile doing it.

HARRY PALMER,
AMERICAN LAWYER

We are more casual about qualifying the people we allow to act as advocates in the courtroom than we are about licensing electricians.

WARREN BURGER,
SUPREME COURT JUSTICE

Most lawyers, it seems to me, simply can't balance their energies: the goal of success and more money chips away at them until they have succumbed to a dangerous kind of myopia.

H. JAMES THOMAS,
AMERICAN LAWYER

Heaven help them

Attorney Rodney Donohoo, of Santa Ana, California, was riding up an elevator with two elderly women one day. One of the ladies asked if lawyers had offices on all the top floors of the building.

"Yes, they do," Donohoo replied.

"It's a good thing," the woman told her friend. "That's probably as close to heaven as most lawyers will ever get."

If at first you don't succeed ...

In 1967, Maxcy Filer, then 36 years old and fresh out of law school, took the California bar exam for the first time.

He flunked the grueling three-day test. So he tried again ... and again ... and again. Twenty-four frustrating years later, Filer finally passed – on his 47th try!

"I never once thought seriously about giving up," said the 60-year-old Filer of Compton, California. "I absolutely knew that sooner or later I would pass that exam."

What gave me away?

Convicted con man Peter Horsford, who was accused of impersonating a lawyer, had trouble getting a trial date in New York.

The problem was that four of the judges considered for his trial were disqualified from hearing the case – because he had argued cases in their courtrooms.

"I should have suspected he wasn't a lawyer," said one of the judges. "He was always so punctual and polite."

Legal briefs

Miami lawyer Alvin Goodman showed up at the Metropolitan Correctional Center early one Sunday to see a client. But because the attorney was violating the dress code by wearing shorts, he was denied entry.

Rather than go all the way home, Goodman stopped off at a nearby garage sale. Although there were no pants, he bought a nice turquoise skirt. He put it on and returned to the correctional center.

When the guard balked, Goodman argued that if women wearing pants are allowed inside then men wearing skirts should be too. The guard reluctantly agreed.

Two sides to everything

In the 1920s, a plaintiff brought suit against the City of New York after he claimed to have been seriously injured from falling in an open manhole.

During his trial, Dr. Willard Parker, appearing as an expert witness for the plaintiff, testified that the plaintiff, "had been so badly hurt that he could lie on only one side."

Whereupon the city attorney joked, "I suppose, doctor, you mean he would make a very poor lawyer?"

When worlds collide

In 1988, Laramie, Wyoming, attorney Becky Klemt wrote letters to several attorneys in California offering a job to collect child support for a client whose husband had moved to Los Angeles.

In declining the offer, lawyer Stephen Corris, who specializes in international trade, wrote Klemt, "Without sounding pretentious, my current retainer for cases is a flat $100,000, with an additional charge of $1,000 an hour."

Klemt then fired off a letter back to Corris, saying in part, "Steve, I've got news – you can't say you charge a $100,000 retainer fee and an additional $1,000 an hour without sounding pretentious. It just can't be done. Especially when you're writing to someone in Laramie, Wyoming, where you're considered pretentious if you wear socks to court or drive anything fancier than a Ford Bronco. Hell, Steve, all the lawyers in Laramie, put together, don't charge $1,000 an hour ...

P.S.: Incidentally, we have advised our client of your hourly rate. She is willing to pay you $1,000 per hour to collect this judgment provided it doesn't take you more than four seconds."

In the name of love

Seattle attorney Jeffrey Leppo was relieved when the judge granted his motion for a postponement of a case he was to argue in federal court.

But then to his shock, the lawyer realized that the new date of the trial fell during his honeymoon. So Leppo filed a motion for a second postponement. Without it, he feared, there might not even be a wedding let alone a honeymoon. Said Leppo in his motion, "It has taken counsel over 34 years to find someone whom he loves and who loves him."

A sympathetic judge granted the motion, and Leppo's wedding went off without a hitch.

CLIENTS

Client, n. A person who has made the customary choice between the two methods of being legally robbed.

AMBROSE BIERCE, AMERICAN WRITER

If you're a litigating attorney, always discuss tactics with the client at the trial. Not only will this surprise your adversary but your client as well.

ARTHUR GREEBLER, AMERICAN LAWYER

Definition of a lawyer's function: To protect his clients from being persuaded by persons whom they do not know to enter into contracts which they do not understand to purchase goods which they do not want with money which they have not got.

LORD WILFRID ARTHUR GREENE,
ENGLISH JUDGE

Praise the adversary. He is the catalyst by which you bill your client. Damn the client. He is your true enemy.

STEVEN J. KUMBLE, AMERICAN LAWYER

I'd rather have my hand cut off than betray the interests of a client.

RAYMOND BURR,
AS TELEVISION LAWYER PERRY MASON

About half the practice of a decent lawyer consists in telling would-be clients that they are damned fools and should stop.

ELIHU ROOT,
AMERICAN LAWYER AND STATESMAN

[The] ideal client is the very wealthy man in very great trouble.

JOHN STERLING,
AMERICAN LAWYER

Don't try to instruct your lawyer. If you do, you've got the wrong lawyer.

JOHN T. NOLAN

An investigation is underway, and for the first time in my life I may actually have to stoop to retaining a lawyer. This is the end of something pure and good. Once a fellow breaks down and hires his first attorney, he has gone and booked himself passage aboard the hand basket to Hades.

TOM ROBBINS,
AMERICAN WRITER

Of course people are getting smarter nowadays; they are letting lawyers instead of their conscience be their guides.

WILL ROGERS,
AMERICAN ACTOR AND HUMORIST

If there is any truth to the old proverb that "one who is his own lawyer has a fool for a client," the Court ... now bestows a constitutional right on one to make a fool of himself.

HARRY A. BLACKMUN,
SUPREME COURT JUSTICE, DISSENTING IN A 6-3 RULING
THAT ALLOWED A DEFENDANT TO REFUSE COUNSEL

Journalists are a hard group of people to love, but they're an easy group to defend.

FLOYD ABRAMS,
AMERICAN LAWYER

Chutzpa is that quality enshrined in a man who, having killed his mother and father, throws himself on the mercy of the court because he is an orphan.

LEO ROSTEN,
POLISH-AMERICAN WRITER

A defendant is entitled to a fair trial but not a perfect one.

U.S. SUPREME COURT

If there were no bad people there would be no good lawyers.

CHARLES DICKENS,
19TH-CENTURY ENGLISH WRITER

Most lawyers who win a case advise their clients that "we have won." And when justice has frowned upon their cause that "you have lost".

LOUIS NIZER, AMERICAN LAWYER

There is never a deed so foul that something couldn't be said for the guy; that's why there are lawyers.

MELVIN BELLI,
AMERICAN LAWYER

Things in law tend to be black and white. But we all know that some people are a little bit guilty, while other people are guilty as hell.

DONALD R. CRESSEY,
AMERICAN WRITER

I don't know as I want a lawyer to tell me what I cannot do.
I hire him to tell me how to do what I want to do.

J.P. MORGAN,
AMERICAN FINANCIER

I get paid for seeing that my clients have every break the law
allows. I have knowingly defended a number of guilty men.
But the guilty never escape unscathed. My fees are sufficient
punishment for anyone.

F. LEE BAILEY,
AMERICAN LAWYER

In former days, everyone found the assumption of innocence
so easy; today we find fatally easy the assumption of guilt.

AMANDA CROSS,
AMERICAN LITERARY SCHOLAR AND WRITER

A woman has a much better chance than a man of acquittal
on a murder charge ... If she happens to be a blonde, her
chances rise about 45 percent.

JOHN MCGEORGE,
AUSTRALIAN PSYCHIATRIST

Fools and obstinate men make lawyers rich.

HENRY GEORGE BOHN, 19TH-CENTURY ENGLISH PUBLISHER

It took man thousands of years to put words down on
paper, and his lawyers still wish he wouldn't.

MIGNON MCLAUGHLIN,
AMERICAN WRITER

He who is always his own counselor will often have a fool
for his client.

PORTFOLIO,
A PHILADELPHIA MAGAZINE, AUGUST 1809

Most of my clients are chastened by having been caught, but often if they win the case, they think they are invincible.

ALAN DERSHOWITZ,
AMERICAN LAWYER AND HARVARD LAW PROFESSOR

When you're a lawyer, you expect your client to lie to you, but not when he is the president.

DICK HOUSER

It is easy to tell a lie, but hard to tell only one.

RICHARD WYDICK,
AMERICAN LAWYER ON CLIENTS WHO FIB

There seems to be a sense in America that we have a God-given right to be idiots and not have to pay for it.

CHARLES SYKES,
AMERICAN AUTHOR COMMENTING ON SUITS FILED BY PLAINTIFFS
WHO WON'T ACCEPT BLAME FOR PROBLEMS THEY BROUGHT ON THEMSELVES

When you believe someone is truly innocent, then the job of defending them becomes more difficult because you know that you are the only thing between them and the jail house door.

RIKKI KLIEMAN,
AMERICAN LAWYER

As attorneys, we operate in a legal system where our stated purpose is to achieve justice for our clients. My clients, however, prefer victories over justice.

DANNY MANAUSA,
AMERICAN LAWYER

I'm trusting in the Lord and a good lawyer.

OLIVER NORTH,
MARINE LT. COLONEL, BEFORE TESTIFYING AT THE IRAN-CONTRA HEARINGS

The specialist

While working as a court-appointed attorney in Fulton County, Georgia, Emory Potter was assigned a client who was accused of criminal trespass. During the pre-trial conference, Potter asked him if he had any prior arrests or convictions. "Yes, sir," the defendant admitted, lowering his eyes. "I've got quite a few."

"Any felonies?" Potter inquired.

"No, sir!" the defendant replied indignantly. "I specialize in misdemeanors!"

Preemptive justice

Years ago in Kentucky, a prosecutor offered to settle the charge in a criminal case if the defendant would plead guilty and accept a five-year sentence.

On the advice of his defense attorney, the defendant turned down the deal and the case went to trial where he was eventually convicted. Before imposing a life sentence, without parole, the judged asked the defendant if he had anything to say.

"Yes, your honor," said the defendant. "You might as well tack on a few more years – because if I ever get out, I'm gonna kill my lawyer!"

The whole truth and nothing but

During a case in municipal court in Middletown, Ohio, a lawyer asked the judge to be excused from representing his client.

The judge scanned the court room, looking for a suitable replacement. But before he could find one, the defendant stood up and said, "That's all right, Judge. I won't be needing another lawyer. I've decided to tell the truth."

Once bitten …

About a year after unsuccessfully defending a client, British lawyer Sir Patrick Hastings found himself cross-examining the very same man in another trial.

The witness was not being cooperative, so Sir Patrick, who did not realize the man was once his client, warned him, "You will answer my questions directly, take my advice."

"I will not take your advice, sir," the witness snapped. "I took it once and it put me inside [jail] for six months."

LAW FIRMS

The screening process through which law firms choose new partners is perhaps as well considered as anything this side of a papal election.

NEAL JOHNSTON,
CHIEF OF STAFF, NEW YORK CITY COUNCIL

Panic is a way of life in a major law firm, and clients like Sonny Capps can cause ulcers. Our clients are our only assets, so we kill ourselves for them.

LAWYER OLIVER LAMBERT,
IN *THE FIRM* BY JOHN GRISHAM

No one is under pressure. There wasn't a light on when I left at 2 o'clock this morning.

HOYT MOONE,
AMERICAN LAWYER

We shake papers at each other the way primitive tribes shake spears.

JOHN JAY OSBORN JR.,
AUTHOR OF *THE ASSOCIATES*

I regret that I have but one law firm to give to my country.

ADLAI STEVENSON,
AMERICAN LAWYER AND DIPLOMAT,
REFERRING TO PRESIDENT JOHN KENNEDY'S REPEATED SELECTION
OF MEMBERS OF STEVENSON'S LAW FIRM TO SERVE IN HIS ADMINISTRATION

Law firms are becoming like professional sports teams – the uniforms remain the same, but the players change regularly.

TERRY CARTER,
AMERICAN JOURNALIST

Law is one of the last citadels of wavering conservatism in an untidy world, and the offices of most lawyers reflect it.

ROBERT TRAVER,
AMERICAN WRITER AND JUDGE

To compensate for minor irregularities in the earth's rotation, official international timekeepers add one second to this day. U.S. law firms adjust their bills.

DAVE BARRY,
AMERICAN HUMORIST

A no-win situation

At an annual Bosses Night dinner for lawyers sponsored by legal secretaries in Helena, Montana, it was time to announce the Boss of the Year. The master of ceremonies began, "First of all, our winner is a graduate of the University of Montana. So that already eliminates some of you as candidates. Our winner is also a partner in a downtown Helena law firm. That eliminates some more of you. Our nominee is honest, upright, dedicated ..."

A voice from the audience cut in and said, "Well, there go the rest of us."

At least there's free parking

The following classified ad appeared in an issue of the *Texas Bar Journal*:

"Small, highly disorganized ... law firm, having characteristically waited past the last minute, frantically seeks associate with two to four years of experience in general business representation and business litigation. Successful applicant must be able to function with little or no guidance in extremely chaotic environment, and be able to stand long periods of indecision punctuated by short bursts of frantic activity ... Toleration of tobacco smoke required. Affinity for hard liquor recommended ... Free parking ... Only the stouthearted need apply."

JUDGES

The judge weighs the arguments and puts a brave face on
the matter, and, since there must be a decision, decides as he
can, and hopes he has done justice.

RALPH WALDO EMERSON,
19TH-CENTURY AMERICAN WRITER AND POET

A judge is one more learned than witty, more reverend than
plausible, and more advised than confident. Above all
things, integrity is their portion and proper virtue.

FRANCIS BACON,
16TH-CENTURY ENGLISH PHILOSOPHER AND WRITER

Appellate Division judges [are] the whores who became
madams.

MARTIN ERDMANN,
AMERICAN LAWYER

The right to one's day in court is meaningless if the judge
who hears the case lacks the talent, experience and
temperament that will enable him to protect imperiled rights
and to render a fair decision.

WILLIAM H. REHNQUIST, SUPREME COURT JUSTICE

Judges are, in many respects, like parents. You have to give
them a good enough reason to do what you want.

DARLENE RICKER, AMERICAN LAWYER AND LEGAL JOURNALIST

When did a judge ever think? He's paid not to.

MAXWELL ANDERSON, AMERICAN PLAYWRIGHT,
AND
HAROLD HICKERSON, AMERICAN WRITER

It has been said that a judge is a member of the Bar who once knew a governor.

CURTIS BOK,
PENNSYLVANIA SUPREME COURT JUSTICE

Judges are the weakest link in our system of justice, and they are also the most protected.

ALAN M. DERSHOWITZ,
HARVARD LAW PROFESSOR AND APPELLATE LAWYER

For Heaven's sake discard the monstrous wig which makes the English judges look like rats peeping through bunches of oakum.

THOMAS JEFFERSON,
3RD PRESIDENT OF THE UNITED STATES

The ability of a judge to put himself into the shoes of the men and women who appear before him is the heart of being a decent judge.

JOSEPH A. WAPNER,
JUDGE OF THE TELEVISION SHOW *THE PEOPLE'S COURT*

Courtrooms contain every symbol of authority that a set designer could imagine. Everyone stands up when you come in. You wear a costume identifying you as, if not quite divine, someone special.

IRVING R. KAUFMAN,
U.S. COURT OF APPEALS JUDGE

A judge is unjust who hears but one side of a case, even though he decides it justly.

SENECA,
1ST-CENTURY B.C. ROMAN STATESMAN AND PHILOSOPHER

I'll have you understand I am running this court, and the law hasn't got a damn thing to do with it!

SAM ERVIN,
UNITED STATES SENATOR,
RECALLING AN OLD MAGISTRATE'S WORDS TO A YOUNG ATTORNEY

There are no more reactionary people in the world than judges.

NIKOLAI LENIN,
RUSSIAN REVOLUTIONARY LEADER

There should be many judges, for few will always do the will of few.

NICCOLO MACHIAVELLI,
15TH-CENTURY ITALIAN STATESMAN AND POLITICAL PHILOSOPHER

Judge: A law student who marks his own examination papers.

H. L. MENCKEN,
AMERICAN JOURNALIST

The judge is condemned when the guilty is acquitted.

PUBLILIUS SYRUS,
1ST-CENTURY B.C. ROMAN WRITER

The acme of judicial distinction means the ability to look a lawyer straight in the eyes for two hours and not hear a damned word he says.

JOHN MARSHALL,
SUPREME COURT JUSTICE

The thing to fear is not the law but the judge.
RUSSIAN SAYING

The halls of justice. That's the only place you see the justice, is in the halls.
LENNY BRUCE,
AMERICAN COMEDIAN

Judging is a lonely job in which a man is, as near as may be, an island entire.
ABE FORTAS,
SUPREME COURT JUSTICE

I don't want to know what the law is, I want to know who the judge is.
ROY M. COHN,
AMERICAN LAWYER

Judges are best in the beginning; they deteriorate as time passes.
TACITUS,
1ST-CENTURY ROMAN HISTORIAN

A judge is merely a lawyer who has been benched.
CHARLES E. CLARK,
U.S. COURT OF APPEALS JUDGE

I will tell you about judges. You can take the most mild-mannered and tender-hearted man you ever saw, make him a judge for life, and his disposition to tyrannize over people will grow with what he feeds on.
CHAMP CLARK,
UNITED STATES CONGRESSMAN

Knowing that religion does not furnish grosser bigots than law, I expect little from old judges.

THOMAS JEFFERSON,
3RD PRESIDENT OF THE UNITED STATES

The law is relaxed when the judge shows pity.

PUBLILIUS SYRUS,
1ST-CENTURY B.C. ROMAN WRITER

A good and faithful judge prefers what is right to what is expedient.

HORACE,
1ST-CENTURY B.C. ROMAN POET AND SATIRIST

He who has the judge for his father goes into court with an easy mind.

MIGUEL DE CERVANTES,
16TH-CENTURY SPANISH WRITER

The duty of a judge is to render justice; his art is to delay it.

JEAN DE LA BRUYÈRE,
17TH-CENTURY FRENCH WRITER AND MORALIST

The judge is nothing but the law speaking.

BENJAMIN WHICHCOTE,
17TH-CENTURY ENGLISH PHILOSOPHICAL THEOLOGIAN

Judges are apt to be naive, simple-minded men.

OLIVER WENDELL HOLMES JR.,
SUPREME COURT JUSTICE

Judge: n. Ringmaster v. To toss a coin

ROBERT MORRIS,
AMERICAN LAWYER

A lifetime diet of the law alone turns judges into dull, dry husks.

WILLIAM O. DOUGLAS,
SUPREME COURT JUSTICE

A judge should be about sixty, clean shaven, with white hair, China-blue eyes, and hemorrhoids so that he will have that concerned look.

ANONYMOUS

I'm surprised [the judge] doesn't take out a rifle in the courtroom and shoot 'em.

LESLIE ABRAMSON,
DEFENSE ATTORNEY IN THE MURDER TRIAL OF ERIK AND LYLE MENENDEZ,
ASSERTING THAT THE JUDGE WAS BIASED

I always approach Judge [Lemuel] Shaw as a savage approaches his fetish, knowing that he is ugly, but feeling that he is great.

RUFUS CHOATE,
19TH-CENTURY AMERICAN JURIST

I'm a mere flash in the pan. I take solace in the fact that nobody remembers who the judge was in the Lindberg case, the William Kennedy Smith case, the Mike Tyson case … This will all pass.

LANCE ITO,
JUDGE IN THE O.J. SIMPSON TRIAL

A judge is not free, like a loose cannon, to inflict indiscriminate damage whenever he announces that he is acting in his judicial capacity.

POTTER STEWART,
SUPREME COURT JUSTICE

All in all, I'd rather have been a judge than a miner. And what's more, being a miner, as soon as you are too old and tired and sick and stupid to do the job properly, you have to go. Well, the very opposite applies with judges.

PETER COOK,
BRITISH WRITER AND ENTERTAINER

Go ahead ... make my day

When two attorneys vehemently argued over a motion in her courtroom, Providence (Rhode Island) Superior Court Judge Patricia Hurst threatened to shoot them both – with a water pistol.

"I told them I have a good way of dealing with prolonged motions," the squirt-gun-toting judge told reporters later.

Because she was seen brandishing the squirt gun in court, Hurst was suspended for a month. Said Hurst, who surrendered the water gun to her attorney, "I'm probably guilty of having a bad sense of humor."

A fine(d) judge

An Alaskan judge levied a $500 fine on someone he knew better than anyone else – himself!

In 1991, Magistrate Craig McMahon of Bethel was swamped with 150 more cases on the docket than he had the previous year. To make matters worse, he had no secretary or computer. He had to write his decisions on an old typewriter.

Cases piled up and a few got lost on his desk. As a result, two alcohol prosecution cases had to be dismissed because McMahon had not scheduled speedy trials. "I felt pretty bad about losing the cases because of my procrastination," said the magistrate. "So I fined myself."

Short and sweet

Buffalo attorney Leonard Brizdle was arguing a case before New York Supreme Court Judge Carlton Fisher who called for briefs in ten days.

"Judge," said Brizdle, "if you can give me more time, I can write a shorter brief."

Declared Judge Fisher, "Briefs in twenty days!"

A time to rhyme

Michigan Appellate Court Judge John H. Gillis was so inspired by Joyce Kilmer's classic poem, *Trees*, that he wrote this verse in a 1983 opinion:

> We thought that we would never see
> A suit to compensate a tree.
> A suit whose claim in tort is prest
> Upon a mangled tree's behest;
> A tree whose battered trunk was prest
> Against a Chevy's crumpled crest;
> A tree that faces each new day
> With bark and limb in disarray;
> A tree that may forever bear
> A lasting need for tender care.
> Flora lovers though we three,
> We must uphold the court's decree.
> Affirmed.

And pick up your socks while you're at it

San Francisco Superior Court Judge Lucy Kelly McCabe often answered her own phone when it rang in chambers. Sometimes she wished she hadn't.

That's because she occasionally received an earful from chauvinist lawyers who verbally abused her on the assumption that she was, in their minds, a lowly law clerk.

One day, Judge McCabe answered her phone and was given a tongue-lashing from an attorney who thought he was talking to her law clerk. He had just found out his case was taken off the calendar because a declaration wasn't signed. "Why didn't you call me?" he demanded.

"Because we're not your mother," snapped Judge McCabe before hanging up.

Bathroom humor

When Maine Superior Court Justice Francis C. Marsano stepped into the bathroom off his chambers one memorable day, he heard an unusual click as the door closed behind him. The pin attached to the door handle that moved the bolt had broken.

No courthouse workers discovered Marsano before leaving for the day. Because the bathroom was windowless and concrete-walled, the judge was forced to spend the night there, sleeping on rolls of toilet paper.

After a clerk discovered Marsano's plight the next morning, workers used a sledgehammer to free the judge.

How did he view being locked in a courthouse bathroom for sixteen hours? Said Marsano, "It puts a whole different spin on 'judicial seclusion.'"

F. E. Smith

F. E. Smith, 1st Earl of Birkenhead (1872-1930), was a British politician and lawyer noted for his skilled oratory, wit, and pugnacious views. Below are some of his most celebrated exchanges.

Judge: I have read your case, Mr Smith, and I am no wiser now than I was when I started.

Smith: Possibly not, My Lord, but much better informed.

Judge: Are you trying to show contempt for this court, Mr Smith?

Smith: No, My Lord. I am attempting to conceal it.

Judge: You are extremely offensive, young man!

Smith: As a matter of fact we both are; but I am trying to be, and you can't help it.

Judge: Mr Smith, you must not direct the jury. What do you suppose I am on the bench for?

Smith: It is not for me, your honour, to attempt to fathom the inscrutable workings of Providence.

Smith to witness: So, you were as drunk as a judge?

Judge (interjecting): You mean as drunk as a lord?

Smith: Yes, My Lord.

Master of the Rolls: Really, Mr Smith, do give this Court credit for some little intelligence.

Smith: That is the mistake I made in the Court below, My Lord.

JURIES

Percy Foreman and I once had an argument as to which of us had picked the most stupid jury. I think I won with one that returned a verdict which amounted to "Not guilty with a recommendation of clemency because of reasonable doubt."

F. LEE BAILEY, AMERICAN LAWYER

Jury duty [is] a bog of quicksand on the path to justice.

SIDNEY BERNARD

In the McFarland case the defendant set up the plea of insanity, and succeeded in proving himself a fool. And he was acquitted by a jury of his peers.

AMBROSE BIERCE,
AMERICAN WRITER

Today, the grand jury is the total captive of the prosecutor who, if he is candid, will concede that he can indict anybody, at any time, for almost anything, before any grand jury.

WILLIAM J. CAMPBELL,
U.S. DISTRICT COURT JUDGE

If the district attorney wanted, a grand jury would indict a ham sandwich.

SYDNEY BIDDLE BARROWS,
THE NOTORIOUS MAYFLOWER MADAME

Juries ... have the effect ... of placing the control of the law in the hands of those who would be most apt to abuse it.

JAMES FENIMORE COOPER,
19TH-CENTURY AMERICAN WRITER

With attractive women [defendants] ... juries sometimes have to be restrained from handing them a medal for their crimes.

JOHN MCGEORGE, AUSTRALIAN PSYCHIATRIST

I never saw twelve men in my life that, if you could get them to understand a human case, were not true and right.

CLARENCE S. DARROW, AMERICAN LAWYER AND WRITER

A jury consists of twelve persons chosen to decide who has the better lawyer.

ROBERT FROST, AMERICAN POET

The average juror ... wraps himself in civic virtue. He's a judge now. He tries to act the part and do the right thing.

JACOB D. FUCHSBERG, PRESIDENT, AMERICAN TRIAL LAWYERS ASSOCIATION

Jury: Twelve men of limited information and intelligence, chosen precisely because of their lack of intellectual resilience.

H. L. MENCKEN, AMERICAN JOURNALIST

We have a criminal jury system which is superior to any in the world; and its efficiency is only marred by the difficulty of finding twelve men every day who don't know anything and can't read.

MARK TWAIN, AMERICAN WRITER AND HUMORIST

In today's world a peer is not a hermit.

NEWTON N. MINOW,
FCC CHAIRMAN AND LAWYER, ABOUT THE JUSTICE SYSTEM'S EXCLUDING
POTENTIAL JURORS WHO FOLLOW THE NEWS

To escape jury duty in England, wear a bowler hat and
carry a copy of the *Daily Telegraph*.

JOHN MORTIMER, ENGLISH LAWYER AND WRITER

I would rather have my fate in the hands of twenty-three
representative citizens of the county than in the hands of a
politically appointed judge.

ROBERT MORGENTHAU,
NEW YORK CITY DISTRICT ATTORNEY,
DEFENDING THE SECRECY OF GRAND JURY PROCEEDINGS

The jury is, above all, a political institution, and it must be
regarded in this light in order to be duly appreciated.

ALEXIS DE TOCQUEVILLE,
19TH-CENTURY FRENCH STATESMAN AND WRITER

We, the jury, find our client not guilty.

VERDICT OF A JURY
IN THE MUNICIPAL COURT AT FORT SMITH, ARKANSAS,
IN A DRUNKENNESS CASE, DEC. 2, 1933

I have what jurors want. They want charisma. They want a
fight in the courtroom. They don't want placidity. They
don't want a one-dimensional lawsuit. They came here for a
show. And they want to do what's right.

PHILIP H. CORBOY,
AMERICAN LAWYER

The jury is a collection of sedentary owls.

ELBERT HUBBARD,
AMERICAN WRITER AND EDITOR

A jury is a group of twelve people of average ignorance.

HERBERT SPENCER,
19TH-CENTURY ENGLISH PHILOSOPHER

It is the "ordinariness" of the jury that finally emerges as its unique strength.

MELVYN B. ZERMAN,
AMERICAN WRITER

When you go into court, you are putting your fate in the hands of twelve people who weren't smart enough to get out of jury duty.

NORM CROSBY,
AMERICAN COMEDIAN

Most often a jury reaches the right verdict even if it's for the wrong reasons.

RIKKI KLIEMAN,
AMERICAN LAWYER

"He said, she said" is enough to go to a jury. There are plenty of people making little rocks out of big rocks right now in the penitentiary on the basis of the jury believing "she said" and disbelieving "he said."

DANIEL POLSBY,
LAW PROFESSOR, NORTHWESTERN UNIVERSITY

Excuses, excuses ...

People will say anything to escape jury duty. Here are a few of the wacky excuses uttered in court:

"I sneeze frequently and my false teeth fly out several feet in front of me, which might be distracting to the courtroom proceedings."

"Due to a bad case of bad breath, I would prefer not to be on jury duty, since I would hate to offend anyone."

"I work nights and I would not like listening to someone else's troubles during the morning hours."

"My diabetic poodle needs insulin shots twice a day."

"I am not God and neither are you. Thus, who are we to judge anyone else?"

Jury prudence

Attorney Richard Glasson of Carson City, Nevada, was defending a slip-and-fall case in Douglas County District Court where the plaintiff's attorney was being especially annoying.

Just before the lunch recess, the jury sent out a note to the court which read: "We, the jury, in the interest of an expeditious trial, and for the general reduction of immaterial and repetitious questioning, do hereby recommend that a shocking collar device be securely fastened to plaintiff's counsel. The control of said device shall be entrusted to a responsible member of the jury panel to be selected following the next recess. We thank you for your support."

Plaintiff's counsel went out in the hall with Glasson and immediately settled the case.

Foolhardy

At the beginning of a trial in the Fourth Judicial District of Tennessee, the defendant stuck by his earlier plea of not guilty.

However, once the jury of eight women and four men was selected, the defendant switched his plea. "Why the change?" the judge asked. "Were you persuaded to plead guilty?"

"No, Your Honor," the defendant replied. "When I pleaded not guilty, I didn't know women would be on the jury. I can't fool one woman, so I know I can't fool eight of them."

Trial by Facebook

A juror in a sexual assault and child abduction case at Burnley Crown Court was dismissed after posting a case on Facebook and asking her friends to vote on the verdict she should deliver. The court had been tipped off that she had asked her friends to decide the defendants' guilt or innocence. She said "I don't know which way to go, so I'm holding a poll". Several of her friends came back with guilty verdicts. The trial continued with 11 jurors, and the three defendants were subsequently cleared.

Indispensable

The Court: Is there any reason you could not serve as a juror in this case?

Juror: I don't want to be away from my job that long.

The Court: Can't they do without you at work?

Juror: Yes, but I don't want them to know that.

WITNESSES

In response to the question: "Is that your conclusion that this man is a malingerer?" Dr. Unsworth responded: "I wouldn't be testifying if I didn't think so, unless I was on the other side, then it would be a post-traumatic condition."

LADNER V. HIGGINS, 1954 LOUISIANA APPELLATE COURT

I think that one of the most fundamental responsibilities ... is to give testimony in a court of law, to give it honestly and willingly.

ADLAI E. STEVENSON, AMERICAN LAWYER AND DIPLOMAT

Lies and liars come in all types of packages. At some point the difference between an honest witness and a dishonest one is attitude. Honest witnesses remember the facts the way they must have been, dishonest witnesses remember them the way they should have been.

ERIC ZAGRANS, AMERICAN LAWYER

If you talk to any lawyer who is honest, they'll tell you they think [unethical coaching] happens, and it happens a lot. It is a very easy thing to coach your witnesses. And if you have unscrupulous witnesses to begin with, that's the only nudge they need.

PORTIA MOORE,
AMERICAN LAWYER

For a plot hatched in hell, don't expect angels for witnesses.
ROBERT PERRY, AMERICAN LAWYER

Hold onto your seat

During a trial at which Carl S. Black was an attorney, an eminent psychologist was called to testify. A severe, no-nonsense professional, she sat down in the witness chair, unaware that its rear legs were set precariously on the back of the raised platform. "Will you state your name?" asked the district attorney.

Tilting back in her chair, she opened her mouth to answer, but instead catapulted head-over-heels backward and landed in a stack of exhibits and recording equipment. Everyone watched in stunned silence as she extricated herself, rearranged her disheveled dress and hair, and was reseated on the witness stand. The glare she directed at onlookers dared anyone to so much as smirk.

"Well, Doctor," continued the district attorney, without changing expression, "we could start with an easier question."

Sleepy heads

Phoenix lawyer Clint Batterton was trying to lighten his cross-examination of an anesthesiologist who was a plaintiff in a securities fraud case.

"I guess that means you and I are in the same business because we both put people to sleep," Batterton joked.

"Yes," replied the witness. "But I wake them up."

Ask a stupid question ...

Counsel: Doctor, how many autopsies have you performed on dead people?

Witness: All my autopsies have been performed on dead people.

Counsel: Was that the same nose you broke as a child?

Witness: I only have one, you know.

Counsel: Now, Mrs. Johnson, how was your first marriage terminated?

Witness: By death.

Counsel: And by whose death was it terminated?

Counsel: She had three children, right?

Witness: Yes.

Counsel: How many were boys?

Witness: None.

Counsel: Were there girls?

Counsel: Could you see him from where you were standing?

Witness: I could see his head

Counsel: And where was his head?

Witness: Just above his shoulders.

D.A. What is the meaning of sperm being present?

Witness: It indicates intercourse.

D.A. Male sperm?

Witness: That is the only kind I know.

Counsel: Are you qualified to give a urine sample?

Witness: Yes, I have been since early childhood.

... get a stupid answer

Attorney: Are you sexually active?
Witness: No, I just lie there.

Counsel: What is your date of birth?
Witness: July 15th.
Counsel: What year?
Witness: Every year.

The Court: The charge here is theft of frozen chickens. Are you the defendant, sir?
Defendant: No, sir, I'm the guy who stole the chickens.

Counsel: The truth of the matter is that you are not an unbiased, objective witness, isn't it? You too were shot in the fracas.
Witness : No, sir. I was shot midway between the fracas and the navel.

Counsel: What gear were you in at the moment of the impact?
Witness: Gucci sweats and Reeboks.

Counsel: Mrs. Jones, is your appearance this morning pursuant to a deposition notice which I sent to your attorney?
Witness: No. This is how I dress when I go to work.

Counsel: And lastly, Gary, all your responses must be oral. Ok? What school do you go to?
Witness: Oral.
Counsel: How old are you?
Witness: Oral.

Counsel: What is your marital status?
Witness: Fair.

Counsel: Doctor, before you performed the autopsy, did you check for a pulse?
Witness: No.
Counsel: Did you check for blood pressure?
Witness: No.
Counsel: Did you check for breathing?
Witness: No.
Counsel: So, then it is possible that the patient was alive when you began the autopsy?
Witness: No.
Counsel: How can you be so sure, Doctor?
Witness: Because his brain was sitting on my desk in a jar.
Counsel: But could the patient have still been alive nevertheless?
Witness: Yes, it is possible that he could have been alive and practicing law somewhere.

THE SUPREME COURT

Who is to say that five men ten years ago were right whereas five men looking the other direction today are wrong.

HARRY A. BLACKMUN,
SUPREME COURT JUSTICE,
ON PRIOR COURT DECISIONS, ESPECIALLY 5-4 VOTES

Something about our courtroom scares lawyers to death. Some fellows have fainted.

WILLIAM J. BRENNAN JR.,
SUPREME COURT JUSTICE

If you took the brains of the majority of the Supreme Court and put them into the head of a bird, the bird would fly backward for ever and ever and ever.

BENJAMIN HOOKS,
CHAIRMAN, NATIONAL ASSOCIATION OF COLORED PEOPLE

They were political animals before they got to the Supreme Court, and they don't change when they get there.

CHRISTINE KELLETT,
LAW PROFESSOR, DICKINSON SCHOOL OF LAW, COMMENTING THAT SUPREME
COURT JUSTICES ARE IN STEP WITH THE POPULACE ON MOST ISSUES

You know, it's almost time to turn back the clock. That's right, the Supreme Court's back in session.

JAY LENO,
AMERICAN COMEDIAN

The people can change Congress but only God can change the Supreme Court.

GEORGE W. NORRIS,
UNITED STATES SENATOR

For the most part ... we function as nine small independent law firms.

LEWIS F. POWELL JR.,
SUPREME COURT JUSTICE

We're all eccentrics. We're nine prima donnas.

HARRY A. BLACKMUN,
SUPREME COURT JUSTICE

We current justices read the Constitution in the only way that we can – as 20th-century Americans.

WILLIAM J. BRENNAN JR.,
SUPREME COURT JUSTICE

If this country wanted its Supreme Court to reflect the immediate social or political wishes of the nation's people, it would provide for the election of the court. And if the founding fathers had wanted it that way, they could have said so – or at least hinted at it. They did just the opposite. They designed a system that tried to immunize the court from the changing moods and passions of the people.

MARIO CUOMO,
AMERICAN POLITICIAN

Our Constitution was not written in the sands to be washed away by each wave of new judges blown in by each successive political wind.

HUGO L. BLACK,
SUPREME COURT JUSTICE

In an era of "sound bites" and instant opinion polls it is dangerous to apply broad labels to a single [Supreme Court] term.

LEWIS F. POWELL JR.,
SUPREME COURT JUSTICE

One puts on black robes to scare the hell out of white people, while the other puts on white robes to scare the hell out of blacks.

MORRIS K. UDALL,
UNITED STATES CONGRESSMAN
CONTRASTING SUPREME COURT JUSTICES AND KU KLUX KLAN MEMBERS

Whenever you put a man on the Supreme Court he ceases to be your friend.

HARRY S. TRUMAN,
33RD PRESIDENT OF THE UNITED STATES

Books? Who needs books?

When the Supreme Court was moved from the old capital of Philadelphia to Washington, D.C., in 1800, the government failed to provide the justices with law books.

Said Robert H. Jackson, author of *The Supreme Court in the American System of Government*, "[That] accounts for the high quality of early opinions."

CODES
OF
CONDUCT

ETHICS

Lawyers know that no other group or profession sets higher ethical standards, disciplines itself so rigorously, [and] contributes so much unpaid service to the public.

DAVID R. BRINK,
PRESIDENT, AMERICAN BAR ASSOCIATION

Nobody has a more sacred obligation to obey the law than those who make the law.

SOPHOCLES,
5TH-CENTURY B.C. GREEK DRAMATIST

In civilized life, law floats in a sea of ethics. Each is indispensable to civilization. Without law, we should be at the mercy of the least scrupulous; without ethics, law could not exist.

EARL WARREN,
SUPREME COURT JUSTICE

An eminent lawyer cannot be a dishonest man. Tell me a man is dishonest, and I will answer he is no lawyer. He cannot be, because he is careless and reckless of justice; the law is not in his heart – is not the standard and rule of his conduct.

DANIEL WEBSTER,
19TH-CENTURY AMERICAN STATESMAN, ORATOR AND LAWYER

I didn't really mean that all lawyers are dishonest. Just that the honest ones are all poor.

ANN GERBER,
AMERICAN JOURNALIST

If young people entering the law are honest with themselves, have the ability to say no, resolve not to serve themselves more than their clients, and commit themselves to the oath of the court, we'll all be the better for it.

PAMELA ANN RYMER,
LOS ANGELES FEDERAL JUDGE

I'm not an ambulance chaser. I'm usually there before the ambulance.

MELVIN BELLI,
AMERICAN LAWYER

The excesses of today's legal system and those who profess to be its servants in fact amount to a serious problem and are at the root of a festering public disrespect for the law.

SAMUEL JAN BRAKEL,
AMERICAN LAWYER

Too many lawyers have forgotten that the main purpose of the law profession is to serve the public interest.

PETER BROWN,
AMERICAN LAWYER

You just had to take the practical view that a man always lied on his own behalf, and paid his lawyer, who was an expert, a professional liar, to show him new and better ways of lying.

JAMES GOULD COZZENS,
AMERICAN WRITER

I don't see why we should not come out roundly and say that one of the functions of a lawyer is to lie for his client; and on rare occasions, as I think I have shown, I believe it is.

CHARLES P. CURTIS, AMERICAN LAWYER

Bar associations are notoriously reluctant to disbar or even suspend a member unless he has murdered a judge downtown at high noon, in the presence of the entire Committee on Ethical Practices.

SYDNEY J. HARRIS,
BRITISH-AMERICAN WRITER

What do you get in place of a conscience? Don't answer, I know: a lawyer.

DETECTIVE JIM MCLEOD,
PLAYED BY KIRK DOUGLAS, IN THE FILM *DETECTIVE STORY*

The ethical distinction between lying to a jury and pulling the wool over its eyes is surely a fine one.

PHILLIP E. JOHNSON,
LAW PROFESSOR, UNIVERSITY OF CALIFORNIA

It is difficult to overestimate how responsible Watergate was for putting the spotlight on legal ethics.

MICHAEL ALAN SCHWARTZ,
AMERICAN JOURNALIST

Just addressed the California State Legislature and helped them pass a bill to form a lawyers' association to regulate their conduct. Personally I don't think you can make a lawyer honest by an act of the Legislature. You've got to work on his conscience. And his lack of conscience is what makes him a lawyer.

WILL ROGERS,
AMERICAN ACTOR AND HUMORIST

Let it be said that we are electing people who … will lay aside their own personal shortcomings and have the inner strength to discipline themselves sufficiently that they do not break the law which they themselves are sworn to uphold.

ED BRYANT,
U.S. REPRESENTATIVE FROM TENNESSEE
DURING THE CLINTON IMPEACHMENT HEARINGS

It is safe to assume legal doctrines that claim to be the offspring of logic are either not proud of or not aware of their real parents.

FELIX COHEN,
LAWYER AND LEGAL SCHOLAR

Helping people is never more rewarding than when it's in your own self-interest.

GREG GERMANN AS RICHARD FISH,
SENIOR PARTNER IN THE TELEVISION SHOW ALLY MCBEAL

Professional discourtesy

George Ade, a well-known humorist in the early part of the century, had just finished a delightful speech at a banquet and sat down to applause from the crowd.

The master of ceremonies, a well-known lawyer, got to his feet, shoved his hands into his pants pockets, as was his habit, and asked the crowd, "Doesn't it strike anyone as a little unusual that a professional humorist should be funny?"

When the laughter from the audience subsided, Ade stood up and told the crowd, "Doesn't it strike anyone as a little unusual that a lawyer should have his hands in his own pockets?"

Nod guilty

Judge James Darrah of the San Joaquin County (California) Superior Court granted a convicted murderer a new trial – because the judge confessed that he had fallen asleep during part of a defense witness's testimony.

Judge Darrah found Tab Lee Bennett guilty of murder. But then the judge reconsidered, and filed his own affidavit swearing he had been asleep for 13 minutes of testimony that focused on the description of the scene of the crime. The judge said he couldn't be sure that nodding off didn't have some effect on the verdict.

Woe unto them

Senator Sam Ervin, of North Carolina, loved to tell the story of a young lawyer who showed up at a revival meeting where he was asked to deliver a prayer. Unprepared, the rookie attorney gave a prayer straight from a veteran lawyer's heart: *Stir up much strife amongst thy people, Lord, lest thy servant perish.*

GOVERNMENT

The more perfect civilization is, the less occasion it has for government, because the more it does to regulate its own affairs, and govern itself ... All the great laws of society are laws of nature.

THOMAS PAINE,
18TH-CENTURY BRITISH-AMERICAN POLITICAL PHILOSOPHER AND WRITER

I believe that the law was made for man and not man for the law; that government is the servant of the people and not their master.

JOHN D. ROCKEFELLER JR.,
AMERICAN OIL MAGNATE AND PHILANTHROPIST

The execution of the laws is more important than the making of them.

THOMAS JEFFERSON,
3RD PRESIDENT OF THE UNITED STATES

The last bastion of protecting everyone's right to freedom is a court of law.

RICHARD ISRAELS, CANADIAN LAWYER

Can any of you seriously say the Bill of Rights could get through Congress today? It wouldn't even get out of committee.

F. LEE BAILEY, AMERICAN LAWYER

Law is not self-executing. Unfortunately, at times its execution rests in the hands of those who are faithless to it. And even when its enforcement is committed to those who revere it, law merely deters some human beings from offending, and punishes other human beings for offending. It does not make men good. This task can be performed only by ethics or religion or morality.

SAM. J. ERVIN JR.,
UNITED STATES SENATOR

From Antigone through Martin Luther to Martin Luther King the issue of liberty has turned on the existence of a higher law than that of the State.

MILTON MAYER,
AMERICAN JOURNALIST

A government big enough to give you everything you want is a government big enough to take from you everything you have.

GERALD R. FORD, 38TH PRESIDENT OF THE UNITED STATES

All associations are dangerous to good Government ... and associations of Lawyers the most dangerous of any next to the Military.

CADWALLADER COLDEN,
18TH-CENTURY BRITISH-AMERICAN POLITICAL LEADER

Proving intent is always difficult. But proving an intent by one person to gratify another is impossible. To give the government the power even to ask the question is to encourage sexual McCarthyism.

ALAN DERSHOWITZ,
AMERICAN LAWYER AND HARVARD LAW PROFESSOR,
ON THE IMPEACHMENT OF PRESIDENT CLINTON

I have come to the conclusion that one useless man is called a disgrace, two men are called a law firm and three or more become a Congress.

ATTRIBUTED TO JOHN ADAMS,
2ND PRESIDENT OF THE UNITED STATES, IN THE PLAY *1776*

Younger people are going to think that Washington is sort of a tragic comedy with everyone sort of doing things that are almost like a bleak carnival that has very little impact on their lives and that is lethal to a democracy.

MICHAEL BESCHLOSS, PRESIDENTIAL HISTORIAN

The government in which I believe is that which is based on mere moral sanction ... the real law lives in the kindness of our hearts. If our hearts are empty, no law or political reform can fill them.

LEO TOLSTOY,
19TH-CENTURY RUSSIAN PHILOSOPHER AND AUTHOR

Government is dangerous, so we have to control it. But it's not a necessary evil, it's a necessary good.

GARRY WILLS, NORTHWESTERN UNIVERSITY HISTORY PROFESSOR

Good laws, if they are not obeyed, do not constitute good government.

ARISTOTLE, 4TH-CENTURY B.C. GREEK PHILOSOPHER

Poetic justice

A federal judge in Cincinnati used rhyme and reason when she threw out a lawsuit that challenged Congress' authority to set aside a federal holiday for Christmas. The suit, filed in 1999 by attorney Richard Ganulin, argued that Congress long ago violated the concept of church-state separation when Christmas became a national holiday. In her ruling, U.S. District Court Judge Susan J. Dlott wrote:

> We are all better for Santa, the Easter Bunny too,
> And maybe the Great Pumpkin, to name just a few.
> An extra day off is hardly high treason;
> It may be spent as you wish, regardless of reason.
> One is never jailed, for not having a tree,
> For not going to church, for not spreading glee!
> The court will uphold, seemingly contradictory causes,
> Decreeing 'The Establishment' and 'Santa' both
> worthwhile claus(es).

Open season on lawyers

Before adjourning its session in 1989, the Virginia legislature jokingly considered a bill establishing a new sport – the hunting of attorneys!

The bill was referred to the state game board for a determination of whether lawyers should be deemed a nuisance species. Under the bill, using cash as bait and shouting "whiplash" and "ambulance" to trap lawyers would be strictly prohibited.

The bill for an open season on lawyers failed to pass.

LAW SCHOOL

Doctors and lawyers must go to school for years and years, often with little sleep and with great sacrifice to their first wives.

ROY BLOUNT JR., AMERICAN WRITER

Be prepared, be sharp, be careful, and use the King's English well. And you can forget all the [other rules] unless you remember one more: Get paid.

ROBERT N. C. NIX JR.,
UNITED STATES CONGRESSMAN, GIVING ADVICE TO YOUNG LAWYERS

Law students are trained in the case method, and, to the lawyer, everything in life looks like a case. His first thought in the morning is how to handle the case of the ringing alarm clock.

EDWARD B. PACKARD JR., AMERICAN LAWYER

Law school taught me one thing: how to take two situations that are exactly the same and show how they are different.

HART POMERANTZ, AMERICAN LAWYER

We must begin to train lawyers the minute they walk into law school to tell the truth. They must immediately begin to learn the business of representing people. They must be assigned cases the first day.

GERRY SPENCE, AMERICAN LAWYER

Law school has been described as a place for the accumulation of learning. First-year students bring some in; third-year students take none away. Hence it accumulates.

DANIEL R. WHITE, AMERICAN WRITER

Good law schools teach you to think like lawyers. But the top law schools teach young people to think; just to think. And that makes a potentially great lawyer.

NORM SHERMAN, AMERICAN LAWYER

Law school attempts to profoundly alter the way you think. A challenging but sometimes wrenching experience.

RAY BROWN, AMERICAN LAWYER

If the weakness of the apprentice system was to produce advocates without scholarship, the weakness of the law school system is to turn out scholars with no skill at advocacy.

ROBERT H. JACKSON, SUPREME COURT JUSTICE

The bar exam is a multi-part torture designed by people whose sole purpose in life is to stem the tide of incoming attorneys.

ANONYMOUS ATTORNEY, ONLINE MAGAZINE *TILT*

There is no better way to exercise the imagination than the study of the law. No artist ever interpreted nature as freely as a lawyer interprets the truth.

JEAN GIRAUDOUX, 19TH-CENTURY FRENCH PLAYWRIGHT

If law school is so hard to get through, how come there are so many lawyers?

CALVIN TRILLIN, AMERICAN WRITER

Leave it to beaver

As a young deputy district attorney in Kern County, California, H. Dennis Beaver was trying a consumer fraud case before Judge Walter Conley. But the judge rapidly grew exasperated with the rookie lawyer's line of questioning.

"If you keep on asking these idiotic questions, I am going to send you some place where you have never been," the judge warned Beaver.

"You mean jail, your honor?" Beaver asked.

"No," replied the judge. "Law school!"

And what about the benefits?

When Judge Richard Neely of Charleston, West Virginia, was seeking new law clerks, he ran the following wacky ad in the University of *VIRGINIA LAW WEEKLY*:

"West Virginia's infamous once and future Justice Richard Neely, America's laziest and dumbest judge, seeks a bright person to keep him from looking stupid. Preference will be given to U. Va. law students who studied interesting but useless subjects at snobby schools. If you are dead drunk and miss the interviews, send letters."

OBEYING THE LAW

The mass of the people have nothing to do with the laws but to obey them.

SAMUEL HORSLEY,
18TH-CENTURY ENGLISH BISHOP

One has not only a legal but a moral responsibility to obey just laws. Conversely, one has a moral responsibility to disobey unjust laws.

DR. MARTIN LUTHER KING JR.,
AMERICAN CLERGYMAN AND CIVIL RIGHTS LEADER

No man in this country is so high that he is above the law. No officer of the law may set that law at defiance with impunity. All the officers of the government, from the highest to the lowest, are creatures of the law, and are bound to obey it.

SAMUEL F. MILLER,
19TH-CENTURY AMERICAN JUDGE

In a democracy only those laws which have their bases in folkways or the approval of strong groups have a chance of being enforced.

ABRAHAM MYERSON,
RUSSIAN-AMERICAN NEUROPSYCHIATRIST

There's a lot of law at the end of a nightstick.
GROVER WHALEN,
NEW YORK CITY POLICE COMMISSIONER

Anyone who takes it upon himself, on his private authority, to break a bad law, thereby authorizes everyone else to break the good ones.
DENIS DIDEROT,
18TH-CENTURY FRENCH ENCYCLOPEDIST

Good men must not obey the laws too well.
RALPH WALDO EMERSON,
19TH-CENTURY AMERICAN POET AND WRITER

Laws were made to be broken.
Christopher North, 18th-century Scottish writer
The best use of good laws is to teach men to trample bad laws under their feet.
WENDELL PHILLIPS,
19TH-CENTURY AMERICAN ORATOR AND REFORMER

To make laws that man cannot, and will not obey, serves to bring all law into contempt.
ELIZABETH CADY STANTON,
19TH-CENTURY AMERICAN SUFFRAGIST

Late every night in Connecticut, lights go out in the cities and towns, and citizens by tens of thousands proceed zestfully to break the law. Of course, there is always a witness to the crime – but as though to make the law completely unenforceable, Connecticut forbids spouses from testifying against one another.
TIME MAGAZINE,
ON THE CONNECTICUT LAW AGAINST CONTRACEPTIVES, 1961

There are not enough jails, not enough policemen, not enough courts to enforce a law not supported by the people.

HUBERT HUMPHREY,
38TH VICE PRESIDENT OF THE UNITED STATES

An individual who breaks a law that conscience tells him is unjust, and who willingly accepts the penalty of imprisonment in order to arouse the conscience of the community over its injustice, is in reality expressing the highest respect for the law.

DR. MARTIN LUTHER KING JR.,
AMERICAN CLERGYMAN AND CIVIL RIGHTS LEADER

It ain't no sin if you crack a few laws now and then, just so long as you don't break any.

PEACHES O'DAY,
PLAYED BY MAE WEST, IN THE FILM *EVERY DAY'S A HOLIDAY*

No man is above the law and no man is below it; nor do we ask any man's permission when we ask him to obey it.

THEODORE ROOSEVELT,
26TH PRESIDENT OF THE UNITED STATES

The notorious lawlessness of the Commander has passed into a proverb, familiar to man-of-war's men: The law was not made for the Captain!

HERMAN MELVILLE,
19TH-CENTURY AMERICAN WRITER

Whether ours shall continue to be a government of laws and not of men is now for Congress and ultimately the American people to decide.

ARCHIBALD COX,
WATERGATE PROSECUTOR, AFTER BEING DISMISSED BY
PRESIDENT RICHARD NIXON BECAUSE HE REFUSED TO DROP
HIS LAWSUIT TO OBTAIN WATERGATE-RELATED WHITE HOUSE TAPES

When the President does it that means it is not illegal.

RICHARD NIXON,
37TH PRESIDENT OF THE UNITED STATES

If Nixon is not forced to turn over tapes of his conversations with the ring of men who were conversing on their violations of the law, then liberty will soon be dead in this nation.

WILLIAM O. DOUGLAS,
SUPREME COURT JUSTICE

The illegal we do immediately. The unconstitutional takes a little longer.

HENRY KISSINGER,
NATIONAL SECURITY ADVISOR AND SECRETARY OF STATE IN THE NIXON
ADMINISTRATION

A man's respect for law and order exists in precise relationship to the size of his paycheck.

ADAM CLAYTON POWELL JR.,
AMERICAN CLERGYMAN AND UNITED STATES CONGRESSMAN

There is no man so good, who, were he to submit all his thoughts and action to the laws, would not deserve hanging ten times in his life.

MICHEL DE MONTAIGNE,
16TH-CENTURY FRENCH WRITER

The President again took an oath to tell the truth, the whole truth, and nothing but the truth. The evidence demonstrates that the President failed to adhere to that oath and thus to his Presidential oath to faithfully execute the laws.

KENNETH STARR,
SPECIAL PROSECUTOR FOR THE WHITEWATER INVESTIGATION

He who lives in solitude may make his own laws.

PUBLILIUS SYRUS,
1ST-CENTURY B.C. ROMAN WRITER

If he who breaks the law is not punished, he who obeys it is cheated.

DR. THOMAS SZASZ,
PROFESSOR, SYRACUSE UNIVERSITY

Laws made by common consent must not be trampled on by individuals.

GEORGE WASHINGTON,
1ST PRESIDENT OF THE UNITED STATES

Rigid laws are brittle, not strong, and easily broken.

THOMAS A. WARTOWSKI,
AMERICAN LAWYER

Perjury primarily and directly injures the body politic, for it subverts the judicial process, and this strikes at the heart of the rule of law itself.

CHARLES COOPER,
AMERICAN LAWYER

What about the tooth fairy?

The U.S. District Court for the Southern District in Ohio didn't believe the testimony of an alleged drug dealer.

In a 1981 ruling, the court wrote, "Defendant and his common-law wife ... had a combined drug habit between $60 and $120 per day. This court, not believing in Santa Claus and having severe reservations about the existence of the Easter Bunny, must conclude that one does not support a wife and three children and a drug habit of some $60 to $120 a day on a $267 per month welfare check."

Fast introduction

Atlanta attorney Dennis Scheib stopped by the prosecutor's office on his way to court to represent a new client in a criminal case. Just outside the office, the lawyer saw two officers chasing a man down the hall, so Scheib joined in to help. The trio managed to catch the man who was quickly subdued and handcuffed. Only then did Scheib learn the man's identity – he was the new client that the lawyer was going to represent.

Winner take all

Attorney Arlo Sommervold of Sioux Falls, South Dakota, was representing a defendant charged with stealing hogs.

After Sommervold put on a spirited defense, the jury deliberated for a short while and then returned with its verdict. The jury foreman announced, "We the jury acquit the defendant."

Sommervold turned to shake hands with his client, who then asked, "Does this mean I can keep the hogs?"

JUSTICE

Wrong must not win by technicalities.

AESCHYLUS,
5TH-CENTURY B.C. GREEK DRAMATIST

When it comes to justice, I take no prisoners and I don't
believe in compromising.

MARY FRANCES BERRY,
AMERICAN LEGAL SCHOLAR AND CIVIL RIGHTS ACTIVIST

But let judgment run down as waters, and righteousness as
a mighty stream.

AMOS, 5:24

Get out of the way of Justice. She is blind.

STANISLAW LEC,
CZECH WRITER

Though justice moves slowly, it seldom fails to overtake the
wicked.

HORACE,
1ST-CENTURY B.C. ROMAN POET AND SATIRIST

The wheels of justice ... they're square wheels.

BARBARA CORCORAN,
AMERICAN WRITER

There is no such thing as justice – in or out of court.

CLARENCE DARROW,
AMERICAN LAWYER AND WRITER

Justice is the end of government.

DANIEL DEFOE,
17TH-CENTURY ENGLISH WRITER

Sir, I say that justice is truth in action.

BENJAMIN DISRAELI,
19TH-CENTURY BRITISH PRIME MINISTER

I tell ye Hogan's right when he says: "Justice is blind." Blind she is, an' deef an' dumb an' has a wooden leg!

MR. DOOLEY (FINLEY PETER DUNNE),
AMERICAN HUMORIST

If we are to keep our democracy, there must be one commandment: Thou shalt not ration justice.

LEARNED HAND,
U.S. COURT OF APPEALS JUDGE

Justice, n. A commodity which in a more or less adulterated condition the State sells to the citizen as a reward for his allegiance, taxes, and personal service.

AMBROSE BIERCE, AMERICAN WRITER

The primary duty of a lawyer engaged in public prosecution is not to convict, but to see that justice is done.

CANON 5, CANONS OF PROFESSIONAL ETHICS

Justice is incidental to law and order.

J. EDGAR HOOVER,
DIRECTOR, FBI

Justice should remove the bandage from her eyes long enough to distinguish between the vicious and the unfortunate.

ROBERT G. INGERSOLL,
19TH-CENTURY AMERICAN LAWYER

As soon as I set myself up as the judge and jury, I might as well be the executioner.

RICHARD ISRAELS,
CANADIAN LAWYER

There is no authority without justice.

NAPOLEON I, EMPEROR OF FRANCE

A right is not what someone gives you; it's what no one can take from you.

RAMSEY CLARK,
U.S. ATTORNEY GENERAL

In England, justice is open to all – like the Ritz Hotel.

SIR JAMES MATTHEW (ALSO KNOWN AS J.M. BARRIE), SCOTTISH AUTHOR

Justice delayed is democracy denied.

ROBERT F. KENNEDY,
U.S. ATTORNEY GENERAL

I have a saying – there's no justice in the law.

ELLEN MORPHONIOS,
AMERICAN JUDGE ALSO KNOWN AS "MAXIMUM MORPHONIOS"

This court will not deny the equal protection of the law to the unwashed, unshod, unkempt and uninhibited.

HERMAN WEINKRANTZ,
AMERICAN JUDGE

White folks don't want peace; they want quiet. The price
you pay for peace is justice. Until there is justice, there will
be no peace and quiet.

**REV. JESSE JACKSON,
AMERICAN CLERGYMAN AND CIVIL RIGHTS ACTIVIST**

Justice and judgment lie often a world apart.

**EMMELINE PANKHURST,
ENGLISH SUFFRAGIST**

The fundamentals of justice are that no one shall suffer
wrong, and that the public good be served.

**CICERO,
2ND CENTURY B.C. ROMAN STATESMAN, ORATOR AND WRITER**

Fairness is what justice really is.

**POTTER STEWART,
SUPREME COURT JUSTICE**

Judging from the main portions of the history of the world,
so far, justice is always in jeopardy.

**WALT WHITMAN,
19TH-CENTURY AMERICAN POET**

Unless justice be done to others it will not be done to us.

**WOODROW WILSON,
28TH PRESIDENT OF THE UNITED STATES**

Justice, though she's painted blind
Is to the weaker side inclined.

**SAMUEL BUTLER,
17TH-CENTURY ENGLISH SATIRICAL POET**

Justice is like a train that's nearly always late.

YEVGENY YEVTUSHENKO, RUSSIAN POET

The achievement of justice is an endless process.

JOHN F. KENNEDY,
35TH PRESIDENT OF THE UNITED STATES

Justice is lame as well as blind.

THOMAS OTWAY,
17TH-CENTURY ENGLISH DRAMATIST

Rather suffer an injustice than commit one.

YIDDISH PROVERB

Every virtue is included in the idea of justice, and every just man is good.

THEOGNIS,
6TH-CENTURY B.C. GREEK POET

Let justice be done, though the world perish.

MOTTO OF FERDINAND I,
HOLY ROMAN EMPEROR

Justice may wink a while, but see at last.

THOMAS MIDDLETON,
16TH-CENTURY ENGLISH DRAMATIST

You may not find justice in the courtroom, but you usually get what you deserve.

DAVID SPICER,
AMERICAN LAWYER

Justice is always violent to the party offending, for every man is innocent in his own eyes.

DANIEL DEFOE,
17TH-CENTURY ENGLISH WRITER

One hour of justice is worth a hundred of prayer.

ARAB PROVERB

Justice is my being allowed to do whatever I like. Injustice is whatever prevents my doing so.

SAMUEL BUTLER,
19TH-CENTURY ENGLISH JOURNALIST AND WRITER

Justice is the great standing policy of civil society.

EDMUND BURKE,
18TH-CENTURY ENGLISH STATESMAN AND ORATOR

Absolute freedom mocks at justice. Absolute justice denies freedom.

ALBERT CAMUS,
FRENCH WRITER

Justice? You get justice in the next world. In this world you have the law.

WILLIAM GADDIS,
AMERICAN WRITER

Whereas in Greek the idea of justice was akin to harmony, in Hebrew it is akin to holiness.

JOSEPH H. HERTZ,
BRITISH-BORN HUNGARIAN RABBI

Justice is the earnest and constant will to render to every man his due. The precepts of the law are these: to live honorably, to injure no other man, to render to every man his due.

JUSTINIAN I,
EMPEROR OF BYZANTINE

The love of justice is simply, in the majority of men, the fear
of suffering injustice.

FRANCOIS DE LA ROCHEFOUCAULD,
17TH-CENTURY FRENCH WRITER

Justice is the only thing that allowed the human race to stop
living as animals and to start living as human beings.

FRANK WILSON, AMERICAN JUDGE

If we do not maintain Justice,
Justice will not maintain us.

FRANCIS BACON,
ENGLISH PHILOSOPHER AND WRITER

The greatest dangers to liberty lurk in insidious
encroachment by men of zeal, well-meaning but without
understanding.

LOUIS BRANDEIS,
SUPREME COURT JUSTICE

Whenever a separation is made between liberty and justice,
neither, in my opinion, is safe.

EDMUND BURKE,
BRITISH POLITICAL PHILOSOPHER AND STATESMAN

They [lawyers] talk about the law – why, gentlemen, it's not
the law we want, but justice.

JOHN DUDLEY,
18TH-CENTURY AMERICAN JUDGE

[The law] is a very imperfect mechanism. If you press
exactly the right buttons and are also lucky, justice may
show up in the answer.

RAYMOND CHANDLER,
AMERICAN WRITER

Justice seems to drown in a sea of "technicalities"... In order to have equal justice there must be some rules which are applied evenly... to all regardless of power, gender, lifestyle, race, etc.

RAY BROWN,
AMERICAN LAWYER

Extremism in the defense of liberty is no vice. And moderation in the pursuit of justice is no virtue.

BARRY GOLDWATER,
AMERICAN STATESMAN

I think that there are certain crimes which the law cannot touch, and which therefore, to some extent, justify private revenge.

SHERLOCK HOLMES,
FICTIONAL DETECTIVE CREATED BY SIR ARTHUR CONAN DOYLE

The United States wins its point when justice is done for its citizens in the courts.

INSCRIPTION INSIDE THE JUSTICE DEPARTMENT BUILDING

Justice is a by-product of winning.

SAM WATERSTON AS JACK MCCOY,
DISTRICT ATTORNEY IN THE TELEVISION SHOW *LAW AND ORDER*

As mankind becomes more liberal, they will be more apt to allow that all those who conduct themselves as worthy members of the community are equally entitles to the protections of civil government. I hope ever to see America among the foremost nations of justice and liberality.

GEORGE WASHINGTON,
1ST PRESIDENT OF THE UNITED STATES

Nothing is to be preferred before justice.

SOCRATES,
4TH-CENTURY B.C. GREEK PHILOSOPHER

When there are too many policemen, there can be no liberty.
When there are too many soldiers, there can be no peace.
When there are too many lawyers, there can be no justice.

LIN YUTANG,
CHINESE WRITER

Habeas corpus isn't just a quaint Latin phrase. It was the
key to my freedom.

RUBIN "HURRICANE" CARTER,
AMERICAN BOXER FREED AFTER 19 YEARS IN PRISON
FOR A CRIME HE DIDN'T COMMIT

House calls

Even though doctors stopped making house calls, Memphis Criminal Court Judge Joe B. Brown always thought they were a good idea.

The former criminal defense attorney had on several occasions accepted guilty pleas from burglars and then attached an unusual condition. Their victims got to drop by the thieves' houses and take something from them!

Brown's sentence was carried out by business executive Lionel Winston, whose housekeeper had stolen from him. Accompanied by Judge Brown and a sheriff's deputy, Winston paid two unannounced visits to the ex-housekeeper's house and claimed two coats that he later gave away.

"I asked [the convict] how it felt to lose a possession and he said, 'Not so good,'" Winston recalled. "I said, 'Now you know how it felt.'"

It takes two

Judge William C. Miller of Montgomery County, Maryland, was hearing a case in which the defendant had skipped his court date.

Miller announced he was going to issue a bench warrant to have the defendant picked up.

"You can't do that," said the public defender. "The man is a schizophrenic."

"In that case," replied the judge, "I'll issue two."

Seeking body and soul

Lawyer Amy Jackson of the Legal Aid Society of Salt Lake City, Utah, was discussing a family law case with her paralegal one day. The client had filled out an application with the legal aid society that stated she wanted "soul" custody.

Seeing the error, the paralegal remarked, "I'm not sure we can get jurisdiction."

Wife sentence

A judge known for his unusual sentences made marriage a mandatory condition in a defendant's plea bargain.

When Kevin Musser was convicted of assaulting his live-in girlfriend, Citrus County (Florida) Judge Gary Graham told him, "You have a choice. Marry the mother of your children and get a year's probation or never see her again and get a year in jail."

Musser chose to be sentenced to marriage rather than the hoosegow.

And Toto too?

Referring to a scene from the classic movie *The Wizard of Oz* nearly got a defense attorney cited for contempt.

During sentencing in a criminal trial in Dayton (Ohio) Municipal Court, Judge Michael Merz read aloud from the defendant's rap sheet, "Convicted of manslaughter in 1957 in Kansas." Judge Merz then asked defense counsel George E. Zimmerman, "Do you have any suggestions as to how we can get your client back to Kansas?"

Replied the quick-witted attorney, "How about if I have him click his heels together three times." Realizing his wit might get him into trouble, Zimmerman added, "Oh, I'm sorry, Your Honor."

"That's too funny to be contemptuous, counselor," said Judge Merz. "Perhaps the workhouse will better suit him for the next six months."

INJUSTICE

When one has been threatened with a great injustice, one accepts a smaller as a favor.

JANE WELSH CARLYLE,
19TH-CENTURY SCOTTISH POET

"No, no!" said the Queen. "Sentence first - verdict afterwards."

ALICE IN WONDERLAND BY LEWIS CARROLL

Extreme justice is extreme injustice.

CICERO,
1ST-CENTURY B.C. ROMAN STATESMAN, ORATOR AND WRITER

We have accumulated a wealth of historical experience which confirms our belief that the scales of American justice are out of balance.

ANGELA YVONNE DAVIS,
AMERICAN CIVIL RIGHTS ACTIVIST AND EDUCATOR

National injustice is the surest road to national downfall.

WILLIAM EVARTS, 19TH-CENTURY AMERICAN LAWYER

Justice delayed is justice denied.

WILLIAM GLADSTONE,
19TH-CENTURY BRITISH STATESMAN

Since when do you have to agree with people to defend them from injustice?
LILLIAN HELLMAN, AMERICAN DRAMATIST

Injustice anywhere is a threat to justice everywhere.
DR. MARTIN LUTHER KING JR.,
AMERICAN CLERGYMAN AND CIVIL RIGHTS LEADER

Injustice is relatively easy to bear; what stings is justice.
H. L. MENCKEN, AMERICAN JOURNALIST

A kingdom founded on injustice never lasts.
Seneca, 1st century Roman statesman and philosopher
One had better die fighting against injustice than die like a dog or a rat in a trap.
IDA B. WELLS, AMERICAN JOURNALIST

It would have cost me more trouble to escape from injustice, than it does to submit to it.
JEANNE-MARIE ROLAND,
18TH-CENTURY FRENCH REVOLUTIONARY

Whenever men take the law into their own hands, the loser is the law. And when the law loses, freedom languishes.
ROBERT F. KENNEDY, U.S. ATTORNEY GENERAL

In our courts, when it's a white man's word against a black man's, the white man always wins. They're ugly, but those are the facts of life.
HARPER LEE, AMERICAN WRITER

The court is most merciful when the accused is most rich.
HEBREW PROVERB

That which is not just is not law.

WILLIAM LLOYD GARRISON,
AMERICAN ABOLITIONIST

If it is of such a nature that it requires you to be the agent of injustice to another, then, I say, break the law. Let your life be a counter-friction to stop the machine [government].

HENRY DAVID THOREAU,
AMERICAN WRITER

Split personality

An attorney representing himself in a suit for recovery of his own fees had his case dismissed because he failed to appear for a hearing in the Los Angeles Municipal Court. He subsequently filed a motion requesting the suit be reinstated because, he said, it wouldn't be fair to penalize the client for the mistake of his attorney.

The defendants filed their opposition to the motion. Alluding to the famous woman with the multiple personalities, the defendants dubbed his argument (which he lost) "the Sybil defense."

You've got him!

During a civil case in Cook County (Illinois) Circuit Court, an attorney was doing a particularly skillful job of cross-examining a witness.

Question by question, he laid a trap that seemed inescapable. When he asked the final question, the judge could stand it no longer. Before the witness could answer, the judge yelled, "You've got him! You've got him!"

The case settled during a short recess.

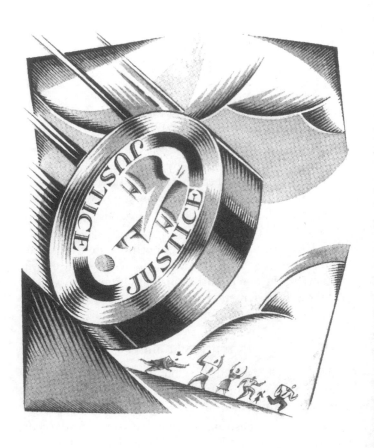

THE
WHEELS
OF JUSTICE

LITIGATION

In the strange heat all litigation brings to bear on things, the very process of litigation fosters the most profound misunderstandings in the world.

RENATA ADLER,
ITALIAN-BORN AMERICAN WRITER, FILM CRITIC, AND PHILOSOPHER

As a people we must somehow get over the notion that the solution to every problem is a lawsuit.

ERNEST CONINE,
AMERICAN JOURNALIST

Criticizing lawyers for lawsuits is like criticizing linebackers for knocking people down.

DALE DAUTEN,
AMERICAN NEWSPAPER COLUMNIST

More lawsuits may not be good for large corporations, but they are good for justice and society, especially if brought by the powerless against the powerful.

ALAN DERSHOWITZ,
LAWYER AND HARVARD LAW PROFESSOR

The courtrooms of America all too often have Piper Cub advocates trying to handle the controls of Boeing 747 litigation.

WARREN BURGER,
SUPREME COURT JUSTICE

To seek the redress of grievances by going to law is like
sheep running for shelter to a bramble bush.

LEWIS W. DILLWYN,
19TH-CENTURY ENGLISH NATURALIST

A lean compromise is better than a fat lawsuit.

ENGLISH PROVERB

The American liability lawsuit mess is the corporate version
of the weather – everyone talks about it, but nothing ever
happens.

THE CORPORATE BOARD

We lawyers know well, and may cite high authority for it if
required, that life would be intolerable if every man insisted
on his legal rights to the full.

FREDERICK POLLOCK,
ENGLISH JUDGE

Never stir up litigation. A worse man can scarcely be found
than one who does this.

ABRAHAM LINCOLN,
16TH PRESIDENT OF THE UNITED STATES

It is becoming increasingly clear that litigation is threatening
our national economic viability. Sheer numbers tell the
story.

J. DANFORTH QUAYLE,
44TH VICE PRESIDENT OF THE UNITED STATES

A simple principle supports the medical litigation industry.
Sue often enough, and eventually a sympathetic jury will
return an outlandish verdict.

LINDA SEEBACH, AMERICAN JOURNALIST

A lawsuit is a fruit tree planted in a lawyer's garden.
ITALIAN PROVERB

The issues can be analyzed in pages less than fifty
If plaintiffs could with thought and words endeavor to be
thrifty.
ASHER RUBIN,
CALIFORNIA DEPUTY ATTORNEY GENERAL, REPLYING IN RHYME TO THE LAWYERS
FOR THE OPPOSITION WHO SUBMITTED THEIR SECOND REQUEST TO FILE A BRIEF
THAT EXCEEDED THE COURT'S 50-PAGE LIMIT

Litigation should be a last resort, not a knee-jerk reflex.
IRVING SHAPIRO,
AMERICAN INDUSTRIALIST

We have too many lawyers chasing too many dollars
through too many endless lawsuits, and that it is time to do
something about it.
CASPAR WEINBERGER,
PUBLISHER OF *FORBES*

Litigation takes the place of sex at middle age.
GORE VIDAL,
AMERICAN WRITER

Four out of five potential litigants will settle their disputes
the first day they come together, if you will put the idea of
arbitration into their heads.
MOSES HENRY GROSSMAN,
AMERICAN JUDGE

A court is a place where what was confused before becomes
more unsettled than ever.
HENRY WALDORF FRANCIS

Discourage litigation. Persuade your neighbors to compromise whenever you can … As a peace-maker, the lawyer has a superior opportunity of being a good man. There will still be business enough.

ABRAHAM LINCOLN,
16TH PRESIDENT OF THE UNITED STATES

Most legal cases are swimming in human interest – like bacteria in a petri dish.

CAMERON STRACHER,
AMERICAN LAWYER

Litigation is a machine which you go into as a pig and come out as a sausage.

AMBROSE BIERCE,
AMERICAN WRITER

Imagine the appeals, dissents and remandments
If lawyers had written the Ten Commandments.

HARRY BENDER

I was never ruined but twice – once when I lost a lawsuit, and once when I gained one.

VOLTAIRE,
18TH-CENTURY FRENCH WRITER

That's not what I pictured

Pennsylvania lawyer James Sposito sued the publisher of a phone book for defamation of character and breach of contract.

Sposito paid for an ad in the phone book promoting his specialty – personal injury cases. The ad was supposed to be illustrated with a picture of two vehicles crashing. Unfortunately, the vehicles pictured next to his name in the ad were ambulances.

Litigating circumstances

The county court in Fairfax, Virginia, had been chosen to test a two-year, small-claims program allowing citizens to file a civil lawsuit for up to $1,000. To keep it a true "people's court," all plaintiffs and defendants represented themselves. Cases were decided rapidly because there weren't many legal technicalities to debate.

In the third week, however, two opposing litigants happened to be attorneys. After the proceedings dragged on for hours, the judge called a recess and stormed into the court clerk's office. "All right," he growled, "who let those lawyers in disguised as real people?

Doobedoobedoo

Attorney:	Do you know if your daughter has ever been involved in voodoo?
Witness:	We both do.
Attorney:	Voodoo?
Witness:	We do.
Attorney:	You do?
Witness:	Yes, voodoo.

Suit yourself

A man sued himself for trying to raid his own trust fund.

Oreste Lodi filed suit against himself in the Shasta (California) County Superior Court. When the judge threw it out, Lodi appealed to the Third Appellate District, which affirmed the lower court's ruling. "In the arena of pleadings, the one at issue here is a slam-dunk frivolous complaint," said the court.

In making the ruling, the court added, "this result cannot be unfair to Mr. Lodi. Although it is true that, as plaintiff and appellant, he loses, it is equally true that, as defendant and respondent, he wins! It is hard to imagine a more even handed application of justice. Truly, it would appear that Oreste Lodi is that rare litigant who is assured of both victory and defeat regardless of which side triumphs."

THE TRIAL

Trial, n. A formal inquiry designed to prove and put upon record the blameless characters of judges, advocates and jurors.

AMBROSE BIERCE,
AMERICAN WRITER

The trial of a case (is) a three-legged stool – a judge and two advocates.

WARREN BURGER,
SUPREME COURT JUSTICE

I love judges, and I love courts. They are my ideals that typify on earth what we shall meet hereafter in heaven under a just God.

WILLIAM HOWARD TAFT,
27TH PRESIDENT OF THE UNITED STATES

The penalty for laughing in the courtroom is six months in jail: if it were not for this penalty, the jury would never hear the evidence.

H. L. MENCKEN,
AMERICAN JOURNALIST

This is a court of law, young man, not a court of justice.

OLIVER WENDELL HOLMES JR.,
SUPREME COURT JUSTICE

This is not a court of love, of compassion, but a court of law.

DANIEL COBURN,
AMERICAN LAWYER

All sides in a trial want to hide at least some of the truth.

ALAN DERSHOWITZ,
LAWYER AND HARVARD LAW PROFESSOR

It's the greatest murder trial of the century – about every two years another one of 'em comes along.

FRANCES NOYES HART,
AMERICAN WRITER

The criminal trial today is ... a kind of show-jumping contest in which the rider for the prosecution must clear every obstacle to succeed.

ROBERT MARK,
BRITISH POLICE COMMISSIONER

Judge: Are you trying to show contempt for the court?
Flower Belle Lee: No, I'm doing my best to hide it.

W. C. FIELDS, AND MAE WEST,
IN THE FILM *MY LITTLE CHICKADEE*

Starting off [a trial] with a completely open mind is a terribly dangerous thing to do.

RT. HON. SIR MELFORD STEVENSON,
BRITISH JUDGE

Trying a case the second time is like eating yesterday morning's oatmeal.

LLOYD PAUL STRYKER,
AMERICAN LAWYER

Trials are the most entertaining of all American spectacles, always better than the theater, and except for a few special cases, much more thrilling than movies.

JOHN WATERS,
AMERICAN FILMMAKER

Can our courts remain completely independent if they become stages for a continuing television series? I think not ... Hear – but we don't need to see.

EUGENE PAVALON,
PRESIDENT AMERICAN TRIAL LAWYERS ASSOCIATION,
ARGUING AGAINST ALLOWING CAMERAS IN COURTROOMS

I'm worried about so much filth and indecent material coming in through the airwaves and through these trials into people's homes. I think the American people have a right to be protected against some of these excesses. While people have a right to a fair trial, I think the American people have an overriding right to let those matters be decided behind closed doors.

GEORGE BUSH,
41ST PRESIDENT OF THE UNITED STATES,
REFERRING TO THE WILLIAM KENNEDY SMITH RAPE TRIAL.

Both consciously and unconsciously, all of the actors in a trial from complaining witnesses and arresting officers through jurors and appeals court judges are frequently and profoundly influenced by race and class.

RAY BROWN,
AMERICAN LAWYER

There is no law in this land about being a little rude in a deposition.

BILL GATES,
CHAIRMAN OF MICROSOFT

In other words

Circuit Judge Ralph Anderson, of South Carolina, showed a love for words as great as his love for law. In a ruling that left lawyers scrambling for their dictionaries, he wrote:

"The evidentiary record consisting of a four (4) day trial is gargantuan, elephantine, and Brobdingnagian... It would be hebetudinous and obtuse to fail to be cognizant of the adverse consequences of a ruling in this case. However, a decision by the court should not be infected with pusillanimity and timidity. The karma of this case must not be aleatory or adventitious, but a pellucid and transpicuous analysis of the law and facts. With certitude and intrepidity and hopefully, with some degree of sagacity, sapience and perspicaciousness, this court disposes of the relevant and germane issues. Autochthonously, this court bifurcates the issues for decisional purposes. The primigenial issue is whether a new trial should be granted. The court comes to this infrangible, ineluctable, and adamantine conclusion that defendant's motion for a new trial absolutely must be denied. The French phrase 'pas du tout' is applied in rejecting the defendant's argument ... I find defendant's degree of culpability to be magnitudinous and megatherine."

The name game

When Jana K. Miller was a new assistant DA working on a case, she ran across the unusual name of Fnu Lnu.

"I tried to check Mr. Lnu on the computer for any previous record, and I was presented with pages and pages of Fnu Lnus to pick from," she recalled. "I told my chief prosecutor that I couldn't figure out which Fnu Lnu to pursue because there were too many to check. Was I embarrassed when she told me that Fnu Lnu meant 'First Name Unknown; Last Name Unknown.'"

No doubt

A defendant was on trial for murder in Oklahoma. There was strong evidence indicating guilt, but there was no corpse. In the defense's closing statement the lawyer, knowing that his client would probably be convicted, resorted to a trick.

"Ladies and gentlemen of the jury, I have a surprise for you all," the lawyer said as he looked at his watch. "Within one minute, the person presumed dead in this case will walk into this courtroom."

He looked toward the courtroom door. The jurors, somewhat stunned, all looked on eagerly. A minute passed. Nothing happened.

Finally the lawyer said, "Actually, I made up the previous statement. But you all looked on with anticipation. I, therefore, put it to you that there is reasonable doubt in this case as to whether anyone was killed and insist that you return a verdict of not guilty."

The jury, clearly confused, retired to deliberate. A few minutes later, the jury returned and pronounced a verdict of guilty.

"But how?" inquired the lawyer. "You must have had some doubt; I saw all of you stare at the door."

Answered the jury foreman: "Oh, we did look. But your client didn't."

The What?

The Court:	I got the Quadrafini, but then he said somebody played in it, and I didn't get that.
Prosecutor:	The Who.
The Court:	The what?

Witness:	Musicians.
Prosecutor:	The Who.
The Court:	Who?
Witness:	The Who. That's the name of the band.
The Court:	So that's the name of the group, The Who?
Witness:	Yes, The Who.
The Court:	Not The What? The Who?
Witness:	No, The Who.
The Court:	You got it everybody? The Quadrafini is a movie with The Who?
Witness:	Punk rockers.
The Court:	Alright.

How many?

Counsel:	Please describe the construction equipment used in your business?
Witness:	Four tractors.
Counsel:	What kind of tractors are they?
Witness:	Fords.
Counsel:	Did you say "four"?
Witness:	Ford. Ford. Like the Ford. It is a Ford tractor.
Counsel:	You didn't say "four," you just said "Ford"?
Witness:	Yes, Ford. That is what you asked me, what kind of tractors.
Counsel:	Are there four Ford tractors? Is that right?
Witness:	No, no. You asked me what kind of a tractor it was and I said Ford tractors.
Counsel:	How many tractors are there?
Witness:	Four.

THE VERDICT

It's like seeing your mother-in-law drive over a cliff in your new Cadillac.

DON BARRETT,
AMERICAN LAWYER, DESCRIBING HIS REACTION WHEN JURORS
FOUND FOR HIS CLIENT BUT AWARDED NO DAMAGES BECAUSE
THEY SAID BOTH PARTIES WERE AT FAULT

The message of the jury sent out basically is that if you don't believe or agree with a verdict, it is OK to go out into the streets, to choose certain fellow human beings, throw rocks at their cars, beat them up and take their property.

ANONYMOUS ALTERNATE JUROR,
AFTER TWO MEN WERE ACQUITTED OF THE MOST SERIOUS CHARGES
IN THE BEATING OF TRUCK DRIVER REGINALD DENNY
DURING THE 1992 LOS ANGELES RIOTS

I think that society is a loser in this case. It appears now that vigilantism is not against the law, at least in some minds. And that's a terrifying thought.

PAMELA BOZANICH,
DISTRICT ATTORNEY AND LEAD PROSECUTOR
IN THE FIRST LYLE AND ERIK MENENDEZ MURDER TRIAL

In America, an acquittal doesn't mean you're innocent. It means you beat the rap. My clients lose even when they win.

F. LEE BAILEY,
AMERICAN LAWYER

We find the defendants incredibly guilty.

FOREMAN RETURNING JURY'S VERDICT ON MAX BIALYSTOCK
AND LEO BLOOM IN THE FILM *THE PRODUCERS*

When we let the victim's personal feelings affect the judge's sentence, we are reverting to a government not of laws, but of men.

HILLER B. ZOBEL,
AMERICAN JUDGE

If it doesn't fit, you must acquit.

JOHNNIE COCHRAN,
DEFENSE ATTORNEY IN THE O.J. SIMPSON TRIAL

We came here in search of justice. You will have to be the judge as to whether or not any of us found it today. But I'm not bitter and I'm not angry.

CHRISTOPHER DARDEN,
PROSECUTOR IN THE O.J. SIMPSON TRIAL AFTER SIMPSON WAS ACQUITTED

It is clear to me that this was an emotional trial and apparently their [the jurors'] decision was based on emotion that overcame reason.

GIL GARCETTI,
LOS ANGELES DISTRICT ATTORNEY AFTER
O.J. SIMPSON WAS ACQUITTED OF MURDER

Coke and bull story

During an Oakland County (California) drug trial, defendant Christopher Plovic claimed that he had been searched improperly by the police. While proving his point, he handed his jacket to Judge Barry Howard.

That turned out to be a big mistake. To everyone's surprise, Judge Howard pulled out a packet of cocaine from Plovic's jacket pocket. Declared the judge, "The only thing comparable is giving a speech at your high school reunion and not realizing your zipper is down."

Coughing up courtroom confusion

A courtroom cough nearly sent an innocent man to prison in Wales because the judge misheard the verdict.

Alan Rashid, 32, was being tried with making a deadly threat. As the foreman of the jury at Cardiff Crown Court rose to deliver a "not guilty" verdict, a fellow juror cleared his throat.

Judge Michael Gibbon clearly heard "guilty" but the "not" was obscured by the cough, so he sentenced Rashid to two years in prison. As Rashid was escorted to his cell to begin the sentence, a confused juror asked the bailiff why the defendant had been jailed after being found not guilty.

Until the juror spoke up, his colleagues had thought Rashid was being sentenced for another crime. The attorneys and the judge then huddled with the court reporter to correct the injustice.

In a case believed to be the first of its kind in Britain, Rashid was led back to the dock and told by Judge Gibbon that he was free to go.

CLOSING
ARGUMENTS

THE PROFESSION

Any culture that has had its Jeffersons, Lincolns and Darrows also must have a healthy notion of the lawyer's role in society.

MATTHEW HODEL,
AMERICAN LAWYER

Ours is a learned profession, not a mere money-getting trade.

AMERICAN BAR ASSOCIATION COMMITTEE
ON PROFESSIONAL ETHICS AND GRIEVANCES, 1943

I have watched with great sadness the decline in esteem held by our society of lawyers. There must be a rediscovery of civility in the profession.

SANDRA DAY O'CONNOR,
SUPREME COURT JUSTICE

Lawyers are given a place of privilege in this society. They are allowed to toil in the majestic edifice of law. This provides them with dignity, challenging work, social power – and often an excellent income. For those privileges, the least they can do is behave with respect toward the institution that gives meaning to their lives: the law.

JOSEPH WAPNER,
JUDGE OF THE TELEVISION SHOW *THE PEOPLE'S COURT*

Those who are concerned about the public image of our profession would do well to look at some of this shoddy advertising.

EDWARD F. SHEA JR.,
AMERICAN LAWYER

Any profession that suffers from so foul a reputation must, in some way, provoke it.

ALAN DERSHOWITZ,
LAWYER AND HARVARD LAW PROFESSOR

To a large extent, lawyers have shed traditional professional qualities, and the law has become an ordinary trade whose success is measured by profits.

PETER BROWN,
AMERICAN LAWYER

My generation and those older than I looked at law as a profession. Too many of the younger ones look at law as a business.

PAMELA ANN RYMER,
LOS ANGELES FEDERAL JUDGE

Lawyer bashing is almost as American as apple pie; everyone knows a good lawyer joke. And for every good lawyer joke, everyone probably knows at least one bad lawyer.

TODD GREER,
LAW STUDENT, UNIVERSITY OF ARKANSAS

Lawyers as a group are no more dedicated to justice or public service than a private public utility is dedicated to giving light.

DAVID MELLINKOFF,
LAW PROFESSOR, UCLA

No other profession is subject to the public contempt and derision that sometimes befalls lawyers... the bitter fruit of public incomprehension of the law itself and its dynamics.

IRVING R. KAUFMAN,
U.S. COURT OF APPEALS JUDGE

More Americans are terrified of being bit, bashed or brutalized by attorneys. No wonder they vent their anxiety in cathartic one-liners. Should we non-lawyers stop telling the one about the skid marks, or the good start, or the researchers who turned to dissecting lawyers because they got emotionally attached to white rats?

WALTER K. OLSON,
SENIOR FELLOW, MANHATTAN INSTITUTE

It is pretty hard to find a group less concerned with serving society and more concerned with serving themselves than the lawyers.

FRED RODELL,
LAW PROFESSOR, YALE UNIVERSITY

Lawyers are like beavers: they get in the mainstream and damn it up.

JOHN NAISBITT,
AMERICAN WRITER

It's not a profession at all, but rather a business service station and repair shop.

ADLAI STEVENSON,
AMERICAN LAWYER AND DIPLOMAT

The law is the only profession which records its mistakes carefully, exactly as they occurred, and yet does not identify them as mistakes.

ELLIOTT DUNLAP SMITH, AMERICAN WRITER

Doctors ... still retain a high degree of public confidence
because they are perceived as healers. Should lawyers not be
healers? Healers, not warriors? Healers, not procurers?
Healers, not hired guns?

WARREN BURGER, SUPREME COURT JUSTICE

Nothing could be more boring than an absolutely accurate
movie about the law.

ROGER EBERT, AMERICAN FILM CRITIC

If it's the last thing I do, I'll put you out of business. There
must be a law even for lawyers.

CORA SMITH,
PLAYED BY ACTRESS LANA TURNER,
IN THE FILM *THE POSTMAN ALWAYS RINGS TWICE*

Of course had you gone to law school like your father, and I
wanted you to, your behavior would've been legal.

MOTHER TALKING TO CONVICT SON IN JAIL
IN CARTOONIST WILEY'S STRIP *NON SEQUITUR*

As a profession we have become afraid of our clients, much
like parents who don't discipline their children.

JOE CONDO, AMERICAN LAWYER

The business of the law is to make sense of the confusion of
what we call human life – to reduce it to order but at the
same time to give it possibility, scope, even dignity.

ARCHIBALD MACLEISH, AMERICAN POET

Ambition within our profession clearly has the potential to
take on an addictive nature.

MIKE PAPANTONIO,
AMERICAN LAWYER

It is hard to say whether the doctors of law or of divinity have made the greater advances in the lucrative business of mystery.

SAMUEL GOLDWYN,
MOVIE PRODUCER

Personally, I don't think you can make a lawyer honest by an act of the legislature. You've got to work on his conscience. And his lack of a conscience is what makes him a lawyer.

WILL ROGERS,
AMERICAN HUMORIST

"Of course I've got lawyers. They are like nuclear weapons. I've got 'em 'cuz everyone else has 'em. But as soon as you use 'em, they mess everything up."

DANNY DE VITO AS LAWRENCE GARFIELD,
CORPORATE RAIDER IN THE FILM OTHER PEOPLE'S MONEY

It's time filmmakers get off their high horse and start creating attorneys fairly and the law honestly. Only then will the public come to understand that perhaps the law is not an ass, nor likewise its practitioners.

ANONYMOUS ATTORNEY,
ONLINE MAGAZINE *TILT*

The law is half-assed, but it's better than working like a horse for minimum wage.

ANONYMOUS ATTORNEY,
ONLINE MAGAZINE *TILT*

Lawyers who use plain language know it doesn't just make good sense, it makes good cents.

CHRISTOPHER BALMFORD,
AUSTRALIAN LAWYER

Legalese persists for a lot of bad reasons – habit, inertia, fear of change, the overwhelming influence of poorly written opinions and forms, false notions of prestige, and any number of myths about plain language … There are enormous social costs of poor legal and official writing.

JOSEPH KIMBLE,
PROFESSOR, THOMAS M. COOLEY LAW SCHOOL

Thanks, Mom

Arnold Berwick worked hard to build up his law practice and earn the respect of his peers and his clients. When his father passed away, Berwick took over his mother's financial affairs, handling her investments and paying her bills.

One day in Saratoga, California, she let her son know how much she appreciated his help. "It's so nice that you're taking care of everything for me," she told him. "Otherwise, I'd have to hire a real attorney."

No respect

Public defenders don't get any respect. While working as an assistant state's attorney in Marathon, Florida, Omar Hechavarria received a telephone call that left him scratching his head and laughing at the same time. On the other end of the line was a woman who wanted to speak to the "public offender."

In another example of no respect, Mark A. Cooper, a public defender in Punta Gorda, Florida, was about to sign a pre-sentence investigation report when he noticed a slight mistake. The report had listed him as a "Public Defendant."

And now the good news …

To help restore the poor public image of the legal profession, a Beverly Hills newspaper came up with a new feature in 1989 and asked for readers' assistance.

"We would be most grateful to receive any good news about things the lawyers have done, and we promise to print them in this new column," said the paper.

The editors waited and waited for someone, anyone, to respond. Exasperated, the paper finally squashed its own idea by running the headline, "Great Deeds by the Attorneys" over an empty space.

A is for Absurd

Everyone who has scanned the Yellow Pages knows the lengths to which businesses will go to get the first listing in their category. Attorneys have tried to get into the act too. For example:

- A Abiding Aggressive Attorney Doug Andrews, Savannah, Georgia
- A Guy Who's a Lawyer, Joseph K. Luby,
- A. Aardvark Accidents Advocacy Office of Cahen, Stephen, P.A., Miami
- AAA Able And Willing Attorneys, West Palm Beach, Florida

LEGAL FEES

A lawyer's opinion is worth nothing unless paid for.
ENGLISH PROVERB

Lawyer to potential client: You have a pretty good case, Mr.
Pitkin. How much justice can you afford?
CARTOON CAPTAIN BY J.B. HANDELSMAN, *THE NEW YORKER*

It is not unprofessional to give free legal advice, but
advertising that the first visit will be free is a bit like a fox
telling chickens he will not bite them until they cross the
threshold of the henhouse.
WARREN BURGER,
SUPREME COURT JUSTICE

A man may as well open an oyster without a knife, as a
lawyer's mouth without a fee.
BARTEN HOLYDAY,
17TH-CENTURY ENGLISH TRANSLATOR

A shell for thee
And a shell for thee
But the oyster is the lawyer's fee.
THOMAS LEWIS INGRAM

Do you mean to say I would be more noble if I charged less?
Where's the nobility in that?

RICHARD ISRAELS,
CANADIAN LAWYER

The public needs the equivalent of Chevrolets as well as
Cadillacs.

LEARNED HAND,
U.S. COURT OF APPEALS JUDGE,
ON THE TREND TOWARD POPULAR MARKETING OF LEGAL SERVICES

I can think of no other business where you are rewarded for
inefficiency. No matter what you sell, the fewer hours of
labor that go into the product, the more you make. With
lawyers it's backwards – the more time you take, the more
inefficient you are, the greater your profit.

ALAN LIEBOWITZ,
LAW FIRM AUDITOR

It seems for a lot of lawyers, padding the bill is a creative
challenge.

DIANE SAWYER,
AMERICAN TELEVISION JOURNALIST

Always remember that when you go into an attorney's
office, you will have to pay for it, first or last.

ANTHONY TROLLOPE,
19TH-CENTURY ENGLISH WRITER

The practice of law is necessarily intertwined with the
commercial world. Legal services should be modern,
efficient and competitively priced, but they shouldn't be
driven by the same bottom-libe principles of the corporate
world.

JEFF STEMPLE,
LAW PROFESSOR, FLORIDA STATE UNIVERSITY

Lawyers charge a fortune to handle a bond offering. You know what it takes to handle a bond offering? The mental capabilities of a filing cabinet.

JIMMY BRESLIN,
AMERICAN WRITER

Doctors purge the body, preachers the conscience, lawyers the purse.

GERMAN PROVERB

We never lose. That's why we charge a lot.

LUCY LIU AS LING WOO,
ATTORNEY IN THE TELEVISION SHOW *ALLY MCBEAL*

All one has to do is read the papers and see how lawyers rightly or wrongly are criticized for lots of things, not the least of which are the fees they earn.

ARTHUR F. GOLDEN,
AMERICAN LAWYER

The buck stops here

As a young lawyer working on his first big case, Keith C. Rennie was sitting in Federal District Court watching a prominent attorney question a witness. The attorney was trying, unsuccessfully, to elicit certain information. Finally the judge turned to the witness and asked a question that prompted the appropriate response.

"Thank you, Your Honor," the attorney said. "How is it that you were able to get to the crux of the matter with one question after I had tried three times?"

"Easy," replied the judge. "I'm not paid by the hour."

Advice and dissent

Orville Isom was a quintessential country lawyer who practiced in Cedar City, Utah, from the 1930s to the 1980s.

If a client couldn't afford the normal fee, Isom would lower it, waive it, or trade his legal work for goods and services.

One day a man who owed him a debt came into Isom's office for legal advice. Isom told the client that technically he could get out of the obligation. "But morally you have a responsibility," the lawyer added. "As legal counsel, my recommendation is that you satisfy the debt."

The client rose and walked toward the door.

"Sir, there is a twenty-five-dollar fee for my advice," Isom reminded him.

With a shake of his head, the man replied, "I'm not taking your advice."

So St. Peter says to the lawyer...

In a 1980 gender discrimination case involving lawyers' fees in the District of Columbia, federal district court judge Malcolm Wilkey told the following joke in his dissenting opinion:

"An immediately deceased lawyer arrived at the Pearly Gates to seek admittance from St. Peter. The Keeper of the Keys was surprisingly warm in his welcome: 'We are so glad to see you. We are particularly happy to have you here, not only because we get so few lawyers up here, but because you lived to the wonderful age of 165.' [The lawyer] was a bit doubtful and hesitant. 'Now, St. Peter, if there's one place I don't want to get into under false pretenses, it's Heaven. I really died at age 78.' St. Peter looked perplexed, frowned, and consulted the scroll in his hand. 'Ah, I see where we made our mistake as to your age. We just added up your time sheets!'"

COURTROOM
PERFORMANCE

[A lawyer's] performance in the courtroom is responsible for about 25 percent of the outcome; the remaining 75 percent depends on the facts.

MELVIN BELLI,
AMERICAN LAWYER

Yes, there's such a thing as luck in trial law but it only comes at 3 o'clock in the morning ...You'll still find me in the library looking for luck at 3 o'clock in the morning.

LOUIS NIZER,
AMERICAN LAWYER

Liars are like snakes. Sooner or later they shed their skin. The cross-examiner's job is to make a few small incisions that will help them do this right in front of the jury. Cross-examination is a process in which you loosen the witness's skin.

MIKE FICARO,
AMERICAN LAWYER

Okay, it's smoke and mirrors. So what? You'd be surprised how much of the legal process is exactly that. Just like in Hollywood, image is everything in the courtroom, dahhhling.

DARLENE RICKER,
AMERICAN LAWYER AND LEGAL JOURNALIST

A criminal lawyer, like a trapeze performer, is seldom more than one slip from an awful fall.

PAUL O'NEIL,
AMERICAN WRITER AND JOURNALIST

As long as I'm in that courtroom and I feel afraid, it means there's something in me that's contagious. If I didn't give a damn, I wouldn't be afraid. Fear is a wonderful emotion.

GERRY SPENCE,
AMERICAN LAWYER

The power of clear statement is the great power at the bar.

DANIEL WEBSTER,
19TH-CENTURY AMERICAN STATESMAN, ORATOR AND LAWYER

One cool judgment is worth a thousand hasty counsels. The thing to be supplied is light, not heat.

WOODROW WILSON,
28TH PRESIDENT OF THE UNITED STATES

There are times when it's not the thrill of winning. It's the fear of losing.

ROY BLACK, AMERICAN LAWYER

Our small group of lawyers was up against perhaps the most intense investigation in the history of criminal justice. If we did not have adequate resources, we wouldn't have been able to [win].

ROBERT SHAPIRO,
DEFENSE ATTORNEY IN THE O.J. SIMPSON TRIAL

They [prosecutors] can make Mother Theresa look like a whore. That's what they're paid for.

LINDA COONEY,
FLORIDA HOUSEWIFE ACQUITTED OF MURDERING HER HUSBAND

In hard-fought litigation where the stakes are high, lawyers say and do a helluva lot of things in anger, and only a psycho would view it as heinous! You're not injuring anyone physically. You're not stealing their money. What's the big problem?

MORTON GALANE,
AMERICAN LAWYER

Trial work requires a computer mind that is rapid in the challenge and response. It's like live TV with no rerun. Not everyone has a mental fast ball and those who don't shouldn't try cases.

NED GOOD,
AMERICAN LAWYER

Most of the great trial lawyers I know are very, very scared. Fear, for an actor, stirs you to a greater performance.

ARTHUR LIMAN,
AMERICAN LAWYER

A criminal trial is like a Russian novel. It starts with exasperating slowness as the characters are introduced to the jury, then there are complications in the form of minor witnesses, the protagonist finally appears and contradictions arise to produce drama, and finally as both jury and spectators grow weary and confused, the pace quickens, reaching its climax in passionate final argument.

CLIFFORD IRVING,
AMERICAN AUTHOR

Lawyers have been known to wrest from reluctant juries triumphant verdicts of acquittal for their clients, even when those clients, as often happens, were clearly and unmistakably innocent.

OSCAR WILDE, IRISH WRITER

Lawyers may often do well, but not often by doing good ...
even when they try.

CHARLES SHERMAN,
AMERICAN LAWYER

Lawyers earn their living by the sweat of browbeating
others.

JAMES GIBBONS HANEKER

Too many lawyers use words on steroids - artificially
puffed-up ways of expressing ideas.

BRYAN GARNER,
EDITOR-IN-CHIEF, *BLACK'S LAW DICTIONARY*

And no dessert, either

In the eyes of some juries, the plaintiffs and defendants act like a bunch of spoiled children.

Such was the case in Jasper, Georgia, when a man was on trial for disorderly conduct after calling a tax assessor a liar.Refusing to render a verdict in the case, the annoyed jury issued a statement that read: "We strongly feel that all parties involved in this case should be sent to bed without supper and not allowed to watch television for a week."

Plaid plead

While covering a trial in 1970, Seattle reporter Eldon Barrett arrived in Superior Court Judge Henry Clay Agnew's court wearing a bright-red, Scottish plaid jacket.

Midway through the afternoon session, Agnew, who was known for running a conservative courtroom, beckoned

Barrett to the bench. In a resounding whisper, the judge told the reporter, "Next time, wear something less loud in court."

"But, Your Honor," Barrett replied smugly, "I thought Justice was blind."

"She is, young man," Agnew said. "But not by any stretch of the imagination is she deaf."

A sick defense

Near the end of a lengthy bench trial in federal district court in Chicago, defense attorney William Levinson moved for a new trial—because of his own inadequate representation.

In the judge's chambers, Levinson labeled his direct examination of his client "a horror." The attorney claimed it was because he was suffering from the flu.

Presiding Judge Ann Williams denied the ill-founded motion.

THE SYSTEM

I have spent all my life under a Communist regime, and I will tell you that a society without any objective legal scale is a terrible one indeed. But a society with no other scale but the legal one is not quite worthy of man either.

ALEXANDER SOLZHENITSYN,
RUSSIAN WRITER

Adversary procedure has served as a guardian of individual liberty since its inception.

STEPHAN LANDSMAN,
LAW PROFESSOR, MARSHALL COLLEGE

The legal system is often a mystery, and we, its priests, preside over rituals baffling to everyday citizens.

HENRY G. MILLER,
PRESIDENT, NEW YORK STATE BAR ASSOCIATION

When Americans leave a courtroom feeling that their cries have been heard, we should all share pride in the fact that our legal system works as well as it does.

JOSEPH WAPNER,
JUDGE OF THE TELEVISION SHOW *THE PEOPLE'S COURT*

Of course there's a different law for the rich and the poor; otherwise, who would go into business?

E. RALPH STEWART

In Germany, under the law everything is prohibited except that which is permitted. In France, under the law everything is permitted except that which is prohibited. In the Soviet Union, everything is prohibited, including that which is permitted. And in Italy, under the law everything is permitted, especially that which is prohibited.

NEWTON MINOW,
FCC CHAIRMAN AND LAWYER

If one man can be allowed to determine for himself what is law, every man can. That means first chaos, then tyranny. Legal process is an essential part of the democratic process.

FELIX FRANKFURTER,
SUPREME COURT JUSTICE

The judicial system is the most expensive machine ever invented for finding out what happened and what to do about it.

IRVING R. KAUFMAN,
U.S. COURT OF APPEALS JUDGE

Before going to prison I believed that criticism of the criminal justice system for its treatment of the poor was so much liberal bleating and bunk. I was wrong.

G. GORDON LIDDY,
CONVICTED NIXON PRESIDENTIAL AIDE

This is what has to be remembered about the law: Beneath that cold, harsh, impersonal exterior there beats a cold, harsh, impersonal heart.

DAVID FROST,
BRITISH TELEVISION JOURNALIST

The law is above the law, you know.

DOROTHY SALISBURY DAVIS, AMERICAN WRITER

If I did half of the things this sorry President [Nixon] did, they would put me under the jail and send every key to the moon. They have the little punishments for the big men and the heavy chastisement for the poor.

RUTH SHAYS,
QUOTED IN *DRYLONGSO* BY JOHN GWALTNEY

The United States is the greatest law factory the world has ever known.

CHARLES EVANS HUGHES,
SUPREME COURT JUSTICE

As tort law operates now, it is more like a lottery than like a rational system of justice.

MICHAEL KINSLEY, AMERICAN JOURNALIST

Our system of civil justice is, at times, a self-inflicted competitive disadvantage.

J. DANFORTH QUAYLE,
44TH VICE PRESIDENT OF THE UNITED STATES

We're doing this whole thing backward. Attorneys should wear numbers on their backs, and box scores should have entries for writs, dispositions and appeals.

BILL VEECK,
OWNER, CHICAGO WHITE SOX

It is better to risk saving a guilty man than to condemn an innocent one.

VOLTAIRE,
18TH-CENTURY FRENCH WRITER

People say law but they mean wealth.

RALPH WALDO EMERSON,
19TH-CENTURY AMERICAN WRITER AND POET

I use the rules to frustrate the law. But I didn't set up the ground rules.

F. LEE BAILEY, AMERICAN LAWYER

This case proves that our justice system works – if you have the money and the influence to go all the way.

ROBERT ARUM,
LAWYER AND LONG TIME ASSOCIATE OF MUHAMMAD ALI,
WHEN THE SUPREME COURT REVERSED ALI'S CONVICTION FOR DRAFT EVASION

There is far too much law for those who can afford it and far too little for those who cannot.

DEREK C. BOK,
PRESIDENT, HARVARD UNIVERSITY

In law, nothing is certain but the expense.

SAMUEL BUTLER,
17TH-CENTURY ENGLISH WRITER

Laws grind the poor, and rich men rule the law.

OLIVER GOLDSMITH,
18TH-CENTURY ENGLISH WRITER

A poor man may still be able to get into heaven, but after Reaganization, he may not be able to get into court.

JANE BRYANT QUINN,
AMERICAN JOURNALIST

An incompetent attorney can delay a trial for years or months. A competent attorney can delay one even longer.

EVELLE J. YOUNGER, AMERICAN LAWYER

America is the paradise of lawyers.

DAVID J. BREWER,
SUPREME COURT JUSTICE

Woman was and is condemned to a system under which the lawful rapes exceed the unlawful ones a million to one.

MARGARET SANGER,
AMERICAN POLITICAL ACTIVIST

I wept for this little girl's lost childhood. I wept for Thomas Jefferson, George Washington, John Adams and all of our brave forefathers ... And most of all, I wept for the fact that our laws have become an object of disrespect, a paper tiger that no longer insures or gives adequate redress to the most elemental right of all to live in peace and relative freedom from fear of those who would violate those laws.

EDWARD A. MILLER,
FLORIDA JUDGE, AFTER BEING FORCED BY LAW TO REDUCE A RAPIST'S SENTENCE

The plain truth of the matter is that rather than alter a system that has now proven without a doubt to be incapable of dealing with crime, our society has altered itself and ignored the problem by sticking our heads in the sand like the proverbial ostrich until he wound up in the belly of a lion.

EDWARD A. MILLER,
FLORIDA JUDGE, IN A LETTER TO THE EDITOR,
WHICH LED TO A REPRIMAND FROM THE FLORIDA SUPREME COURT

It isn't the bad lawyers who are screwing up the justice system in this country, it's the good lawyers. If you have two competent lawyers on opposite sides, a trial that should take three days could easily last six months.

ART BUCHWALD,
AMERICAN JOURNALIST

Law is a reflection and a source of prejudice. It both enforces and suggests forms of bias.

DIANE B. SCHULDER,
AMERICAN LAWYER AND EDUCATOR

Ours is a prostitute society. The system of justice, and most especially the legal profession, is a whorehouse serving those best able to afford the luxuries of justice offered to preferred customers. The lawyer, in these terms, is analogous to a prostitute. The difference between the two is simple. The prostitute is honest – the buck is her aim. The lawyer is dishonest – he claims that justice, service to mankind is his primary purpose. The lawyer's deception of the people springs from his actual money-making role; he represents the client who puts the highest fee on the table.

FLORYNCE RAE KENNEDY,
AMERICAN LAWYER AND CIVIL RIGHTS ACTIVIST

Justice is a system of revenge wherein the State imitates the criminal.

ELBERT HUBBARD,
AMERICAN WRITER AND EDITOR

To be a trial lawyer is to see the ignominy of slow justice in a system in which the process itself punishes all who come in contact with it – the winner as well as the loser.

JOHN A. JENKINS,
JOURNALIST AND LEGAL WRITER

I cannot believe that a republic could hope to exist at the present time, if the influence of lawyers in public business did not increase in proportion to the power of the people.

ALEXIS DE TOCQUEVILLE,
19TH-CENTURY FRENCH STATESMAN AND WRITER

We've produced a system of ending disputes rather than digging up truths.

THOMAS H. ALLEN,
AMERICAN LAWYER

By the argument of counsel it was shown that at half-past ten in the morning on the day of the murder... [the defendant] became insane, and remained so for eleven hours and a half exactly.

MARK TWAIN,
AMERICAN WRITER AND HUMORIST,
COMMENTING ON THE INSANITY DEFENSE

I think the law became an ass the day it let the psychiatrists get their hands on it.

LYNN COMPTON,
LOS ANGELES CHIEF DEPUTY DISTRICT ATTORNEY, AT THE SUMMATION
OF SIRHAN SIRHAN'S TRIAL FOR ASSASSINATING ROBERT F. KENNEDY

An appeal, Hinnissy, is where ye ask wan coort to show its contempt f'r another coort.

MR. DOOLEY (FINLEY PETER DUNNE),
AMERICAN HUMORIST

Please don't let this [not guilty verdict] make you lose faith in our system. Please don't let this deter you from doing a job you're so well qualified to do.

MARCIA CLARK,
LEAD PROSECUTOR IN THE O.J. SIMPSON TRIAL,
TO HER FELLOW ATTORNEYS

The impeachment power is like the ax behind the glass that says, "Do Not Break Except in Case of Emergency."

ALAN DERSHOWITZ,
LAW PROFESSOR, HARVARD UNIVERSITY

Prisons are built with stories of Law.

WILLIAM BLAKE,
19TH-CENTURY ENGLISH POET

People resent that O.J. got himself in trouble, and then trashed the nation's judicial system and racial harmony to save his hide.

FRED GRAHAM,
AMERICAN LAWYER AND JOURNALIST

Achieving "finality" in death cases, and doing so as expeditiously as possible, have become the dominant goals ion death penalty jurisprudence.

MOSES HARRISON II,
ILLINOIS SUPREME COURT JUSTICE

A society without any objective legal scale is a terrible one indeed. But a society with no other scale but the legal one is also less than worthy of man.

ALEXANDER SOLZHENITSYN,
RUSSIAN WRITER

The bigger the system gets, the more impersonal the system gets, and the less ability the judges have to hear the same thing again and again and react to it on a case-by-case basis.

DAVID ROTHMAN,
AMERICAN LAWYER

Rather than functioning as a deterrent, the criminal justice process too often operates to reinforce the offender's belief that he can commit crimes with impunity.

JAMES THOMPSON,
ILLINOIS GOVERNOR

Sock it to him

When Ed Koch was running for mayor of New York City in 1973, he went to a senior citizens center in the Bronx.

The candidate was immediately asked about crime and what he intended to do about it. "Crime is terrible," he replied. "A judge I know was mugged this week and do you know what he did? He called a press conference and said the mugging would in no way affect his judicial decisions in matters of that kind."

An elderly woman stood up and shouted, "Then mug him again!"

A ruling that made no cents

After four years of legal wranglings over the ownership of some property in Palmdale, California, a settlement was finally reached in 1992 – but justice was held up over a single penny.

Los Angeles Superior Court officials refused to let the two parties split a $30,832.81 deposit because one party would receive a penny more than the other. Attorneys from both sides offered to toss in a cent to make it even, but the officials insisted on a new formal order.

To satisfy the court finance officer, a new court order was drawn up and sent by messenger to all parties who had to appear at an early morning special court hearing. The legal costs to resolve the once-cent issue: $1,050.

Three Tiers for the Judge

In front of three justices in the Hong Kong Court of Criminal Appeals, lawyer Angus McKay gave three reasons why he felt his client's conviction should be overturned.

"Mr. McKay," said one of the judges, "the first tier of your case is that the identification was wrong, the second tier that the statements should have been disregarded, and the third tier is that the conviction is against the weight of evidence in any event, is that not right?"

McKay couldn't resist a clever reply: "If I have reduced your Lordship to tiers, should I really continue?"

Typos

- A brief said it had an index containing an "extensive copulation of authorities."

- A court paper was addressed to "The Horable U.S. District Judge."

- A notice of appeal ended with "Rectfully submitted."

- An agricultural lease involving demised premises stated the tenant was entitled to exclusive use and possession of the "demised penises."

- An estate plan attempted a distribution of "asses."

ON REFORM

Even when laws have been written down, they ought not always to remain unaltered.

ARISTOTLE,
4TH-CENTURY B.C. GREEK PHILOSOPHER

Law is merely the expression of the will of the strongest for the time being, and therefore laws have no fixity, but shift from generation to generation.

BROOKS ADAMS,
19TH-CENTURY AMERICAN HISTORIAN

The law, like the traveler, must be ready for the morrow. It must have the principle of growth.

BENJAMIN CARDOZO,
SUPREME COURT JUSTICE

To the law we bow with reverence. It is the one king that commands our allegiance. We will change our king when his rule is oppressive.

BENJAMIN HARRISON,
23RD PRESIDENT OF THE UNITED STATES

Nothing is more subject to change than the laws.

MICHEL DE MONTAIGNE,
16TH-CENTURY FRENCH WRITER

Laws should not be changed without good reason.
CHARLES LOUIS DE MONTESQUIEU,
18TH-CENTURY FRENCH LAWYER AND POLITICAL PHILOSOPHER

When I hear any man talk of an unalterable law, the only effect it produces upon me is to convince me that he is an unalterable fool.
SYDNEY SMITH,
18TH-CENTURY ENGLISH WRITER

Somewhere "out there," beyond the walls of the courthouse, run currents and tides of public opinion which lap at the courtroom door.
WILLIAM H. REHNQUIST,
SUPREME COURT JUSTICE, ON THE PUBLIC'S INFLUENCE TO CHANGE LAWS

Law reform is far too serious a matter to be left to the legal profession.
LORD LESLIE SCARMAN, ENGLISH LAWYER

If you got the say-so, you want to keep it whether you are right or wrong. That's why they have to keep changing the laws – so they don't unbenefit any of these big white men.
RUTH SHAYS,
QUOTED IN *DRYLONGSO* BY JOHN GWALTNEY

Law and justice are not always the same. When they aren't, destroying the law may be the first step toward changing it.
GLORIA STEINEM, AMERICAN WRITER AND FEMINIST

We have the means to change the laws we find unjust or onerous. We cannot, as citizens, pick and choose the laws we will or will not obey.
RONALD W. REAGAN, 40TH PRESIDENT OF THE UNITED STATES

Laws and institutions are constantly tending to gravitate. Like clocks, they must be occasionally cleansed, and wound up, and set to true time.

HENRY WARD BEECHER,
19TH-CENTURY AMERICAN CLERGYMAN

Law and equity are two things that God hath joined, but which man hath put asunder.

CHARLES C. COLTON,
19TH-CENTURY ENGLISH CLERGYMAN AND WRITER

The worse the society, the more law there will be. In Hell there will be nothing but law, and due process will be meticulously observed.

GRANT GILMORE,
AMERICAN LEGAL SCHOLAR

The rule of law can be wiped out in one misguided, however well-intentioned, generation.

WILLIAM T. GOSSETT,
PRESIDENT, AMERICAN BAR ASSOCIATION

New lords, new laws.

SIR JOHN HARINGTON,
16TH CENTURY ENGLISH WRITER AND TRANSLATOR

It cannot be helped, it is as it should be, that the law is behind the times.

OLIVER WENDELL HOLMES JR.,
SUPREME COURT JUSTICE

Law must be stable and yet it cannot stand still.

ROSCOE POUND,
DEAN EMERITUS, HARVARD LAW SCHOOL

Petty laws breed great crimes.

OUIDA,
18TH-CENTURY SCOTTISH WRITER

The law changes and flows like water, and... the stream of women's rights law has become a sudden rushing torrent.

SHANA ALEXANDER,
AMERICAN JOURNALIST

It is perfectly proper to regard and study the law simply as a great anthropological document.

OLIVER WENDELL HOLMES JR.,
SUPREME COURT JUSTICE

Every new time will give its law.

MAXIM GORKY,
RUSSIAN WRITER

We must do more to ensure that people without resources are not disadvantaged in courts whether as civil plaintiffs or criminal defendants or even as victims.

RAY BROWN,
AMERICAN LAWYER

I do not think the state should engage in conduct that should be left to a higher power.

CATHERINE CRIER,
AMERICAN JUDGE, ON THE DEATH PENALTY

Capital punishment would be more effective as a preventive measure if it were administered prior to the crime.

WOODY ALLEN,
AMERICAN WRITER AND DIRECTOR

Legaldegook

Here are some winners of the annual Legaldegook Awards selected by the Plain Language Committee of the State Bar of Texas:

• To an attorney who claims his position is supported by a statement in an accompanying affidavit in the case file: "It all fully appears from the affidavit of the publisher heretofore herein filed."

• To an attorney who writes that the pleading may refer to other documents previously filed: "The Court may take judicial notice of such pleadings which are on file herein and such pleadings are incorporated herein by reference and made a part hereof as if copied here in full."

Who do you trust?

When Miami lawyer Stephen Nagin received a call one day from a potential client who wanted a divorce, he was perplexed because he specialized in antitrust suits.

"Why would you call me?" he asked the woman caller.

"Well," she replied, "I saw your name in the Yellow Pages under antitrust lawyers and I don't trust my husband."

Nagin respectfully declined to represent her.

ADVICE TO LAWYERS

I'll tell you what my daddy told me after my first trial. I thought I was just great. I asked him, "How did I do?" He paused and said, "You've got to guard against speaking more clearly than you think."

HOWARD H. BAKER JR.,
UNITED STATES SENATOR

You don't approach a case with the philosophy of applying abstract justice – you go in to win.

PERCY FOREMAN,
AMERICAN LAWYER

Be concise for clients. Less is more. Bravura displays only serve to irritate; brevity is what pays the rent.

JAMES C. FREUND,
AMERICAN LAWYER

Be you never so high, the law is above you.

THOMAS FULLER,
17TH-CENTURY ENGLISH WRITER

When you have the facts on your side, argue the facts. When you have the law on your side, argue the law. When you have neither, holler.

ALBERT GORE JR.,
45TH VICE PRESIDENT OF THE UNITED STATES

When you have no basis for an argument, abuse the plaintiff.

CICERO,
1ST-CENTURY B.C. ROMAN STATESMAN, ORATOR AND WRITER

My thesis is that the truly successful lawyer finds a good heart more useful than sharp fangs.

MATHEW A. HODEL,
AMERICAN LAWYER

There is a vague popular belief that lawyers are necessarily dishonest. I say vague, because when we consider to what extent confidence and honors are reposed in and conferred upon lawyers by the people, it appears improbable that their impression of dishonesty is very distinct and vivid. Yet the impression is common, almost universal. Let no young man choosing the law for a calling for a moment yield to the popular belief – resolve to be honest at all events; and if in your own judgment you cannot be an honest lawyer, resolve to be honest without being a lawyer. Choose some other occupation, rather than one in the choosing of which you do, in advance, consent to be a knave.

ABRAHAM LINCOLN,
16TH PRESIDENT OF THE UNITED STATES

In university they don't tell you that the greater part of the law is learning to tolerate fools.

DORIS LESSING,
AMERICAN WRITER

[Preparation] is the be-all of good trial work. Everything else – felicity of expression, improvisational brilliance - is a satellite around the sun. Thorough preparation is that sun.

LOUIS NIZER,
AMERICAN LAWYER

I used to say that, as Solicitor General, I made three arguments of every case. First came the one that I planned as I thought – logical, coherent, complete. Second was the one actually presented – interrupted, incoherent, disjointed, disappointing. The third was the utterly devastating argument that I thought of after going to bed that night.

ROBERT H. JACKSON,
SUPREME COURT JUSTICE

Never, never, never, on cross examination, ask a witness a question you don't already know the answer to, was a tenet I absorbed with my baby food. Do it, and you'll often get an answer you don't want.

ATTICUS FINCH
IN THE NOVEL *TO KILL A MOCKINGBIRD* BY HARPER LEE

People don't ordinarily look forward to starting at the bottom. While you may be a lowly foot soldier ... no one knows more about solving a problem than the person at the bottom.

SANDRA DAY O'CONNOR,
SUPREME COURT JUSTICE, RECALLING THE DAYS EARLY IN HER CAREER
IN A MALL LAW OFFICE COLLECTING UNPAID GROCERY BILLS

There is always room at the top.

DANIEL WEBSTER,
AMERICAN STATESMAN, ORATOR, AND LAWYER WHEN ADVISED
NOT TO BECOME A LAWYER BECAUSE THE PROFESSION WAS OVERCROWDED

To find real pleasure in the legal life, you need to open yourself to all your sources of potential meaning ... Understanding a client beyond her present legal problem does not detract from the technical job at hand.

STEVEN KEEVA,
AMERICAN JOURNALIST

Extemporaneous speaking should be practiced and cultivated. It is the lawyer's avenue to the public.

ABRAHAM LINCOLN,
16TH PRESIDENT OF THE UNITED STATES

My father told me that all you need to succeed in the law is a certain amount of common sense and clean fingernails.

JOHN MORTIMER,
ENGLISH LAWYER AND WRITER

Wisdom too often never comes, and so one ought not to reject it merely because it comes too late.

FELIX FRANKFURTER,
SUPREME COURT JUSTICE

Accepting representation of another human being is a serious commitment and should always be treated as such.

WARREN ANDERSON,
AMERICAN LAWYER

Courage is the most important attribute of a lawyer. It is more important than competence or vision. It can never be an elective in any law school ... and it should pervade the heart, the halls of justice and the chambers of the mind.

ROBERT F. KENNEDY,
U.S. ATTORNEY GENERAL

A shot glass of facts is worth a tub of law.

WILLIAM F. MCHUGH,
LAW PROFESSOR, FLORIDA STATE UNIVERSITY

For a good time, hire a hooker. For a lot of time, hire my attorney.

PRISON CELL GRAFFITI

When in the classroom or debating minute matters with classmates, it's perfectly fine to "think like a lawyer." But back on the outside, back in the real world, a contract is still an agreement, property is still stuff, and torts are still those fancy little pastries.

ANONYMOUS ATTORNEY,
ONLINE MAGAZINE *TILT*

Court in repose

After a big lunch, Judge George D. Warner Jr., of the Chancery Court in Meridian, Mississippi, couldn't keep his eyes open in court. He realized he had dropped off to sleep when he cracked his eyes open and not a sound could be heard.

One lawyer was looking at him with his notes in his hand. The other lawyer questioning the witness was standing still before proceeding.

Judge Warner looked at the first lawyer and announced, "Objection sustained!"

"But, Judge, I didn't object," the lawyer said.

"Well," said the embarrassed judge, "you should have!"

INDEX

A

Abrams, Floyd (b. 1936), American lawyer, 31
Abramson, Leslie, defense attorney, 46
Adams, Brooks (1848-1927), American historian, 155
Adams, John (1735-1826), 2nd President of the United States, 77
Adler, Freda (b. 1934), American educator, 8
Adler, Renata (b. 1938), Italian-born American writer, film critic, and
     philosopher, 107
Aeschylus (525-546 B.C.), Greek dramatist, 89
Alexander, Shana (1925-2005), American journalist, 158
Allen, Thomas H. (b. 1945), American lawyer, 150
Allen, Woody (b. 1935), American writer and director, 158
Anacharsis, 6th-century B.C. Scythian philosopher, 11
Anderson, Maxwell (1889-1959), American playwright, 42
Anderson, Warren, American lawyer, 164
Aquinas, St. Thomas (1225-1274), Italian theologian, 5
Arbuthnot, John (1667-1735), Scottish physician and writer, 5
Aristotle (384-322 B.C.), Greek philosopher, 5, 6, 7, 77, 155
Arum, Robert (b. 1931), American lawyer, 148

B

Bacon, Francis (1561-1626), English philosopher and writer, 11, 41, 95
Bailey, F. Lee (b. 1931), American lawyer, 32, 51, 75, 119, 148
Baker, Howard H., Jr. (b. 1925), United States senator, 161
Balmford, Christopher, Australian lawyer, 129
Barrett, Don, American lawyer, 119
Barrows, Sydney Biddle (b. 1952), 51
Barry, Dave (b. 1947), American humorist, 38
Baxter, William F. (b. 1929), Assistant U.S. Attorney General, 17
Beecher, Henry Ward (1813-1887), American clergyman, 4, 8, 157
Belli, Melvin (1907-1996), American lawyer, 70, 139
Bender, Harry, 110
Bernard, Sidney, 51
Berry, Mary Frances (b. 1938), American legal scholar and civil rights activist, 89
Beschloss, Michael, Presidential historian, 77

Bickel, Alexander M. (1924-1974), Romanian-born American legal scholar, 8
Bierce, Ambrose (1942-1914), American writer, 21, 29, 51, 90, 110, 113
Bismarck, Otto von (1815-1898), Prussian prince, 1
Black, Hugo L. (1886-1971), Supreme Court Justice, 64
Black, Roy, American lawyer, 140
Blackmun, Harry A. (1908-1999), Supreme Court Justice, 30, 63, 64
Blake, William (1757-1827), English poet, 151
Bleckley, Logan E. (1827-1907), American judge, 20
Blount, Roy, Jr. (b.1941), American writer, 79
Bohn, Henry George (1796-1884), English publisher, 32
Bok, Curtis (1897-1962), Pennsylvania Supreme Court justice, 42
Bok, Derek C. (b. 1930), President, Harvard University, 148
Borrow, George (1803-1881), English writer and linguist, 16
Bozanich, Pamela, American lawyer, 119
Brakel, Samuel Jan, American lawyer, 70
Brandeis, Louis D. (1856-1941), Supreme Court Justice, 4, 95
Brennan, William J., Jr. (1906-1997), Supreme Court Justice, 63
Breslin, Jimmy (b. 1929), American writer, 135
Brewer, David J. (1837-1910), Supreme Court Justice, 148
Brink, David R. (b. 1919), president, American Bar Association, 69
Brougham, Henry Peter (1778-1868), Scottish judge and political leader, 17
Brown, Peter (b. 1922), American lawyer, 70, 126
Brown, Ray, American lawyer, 80, 96, 115, 158
Bruce, Lenny (1926-1966), American comedian, 44
Bruyère, Jean de la (1645-1696), French writer and moralist, 45
Bryant, Ed (b. 1949), U.S. Representative from Tennessee, 72
Buchwald, Art (1925-2007), American journalist, 149
Bulwer-Lytton, Edward (1803-1873), 11
Burger, Warren (1907-1995), Supreme Court Justice, 25, 107, 113, 128, 133
Burke, Edmund (1729-1797), English statesman and orator, 94, 95
Bush, George (b. 1924), 41st President of the United States, 115
Butler, Samuel (1612-1680), English satirical poet, 92, 148
Butler, Samuel (1835-1902), English journalist and writer, 21, 94

C

Campbell, William J. (b. 1948), U.S. District Court judge, 51
Camus, Albert (1913-1960), French writer, 94
Cardozo, Benjamin (1870-1938), Supreme Court Justice, 155
Carlyle, Jane Welsh (1801-1866), Scottish poet, 101
Carter, Rubin "Hurricane" (b. 1937), American boxer, 97
Carter, Terry, American journalist, 38
Cervantes, Miguel de (1547-1616), Spanish writer, 45
Chandler, Raymond (1888-1959), American mystery and suspense writer, 1, 95

Choate, Joseph H. (1832-1917), American lawyer and diplomat, 17
Choate, Rufus (1799-1859), American jurist, 46
Cicero (106-43 B.C.), Roman statesman, orator, and writer, 5, 10, 92, 101, 162
Clark, Champ (1850-1921), United States Congressman, 44
Clark, Charles E. (1889-1963), U.S. Court of Appeals judge, 44
Clark, Marcia (b. 1953), Lead prosecutor in the O.J. Simpson trial, 151
Clark, Ramsey (b. 1927), U.S. Attorney General, 91
Coburn, Daniel (b. 1943), American lawyer, 114
Cochran, Johnnie (1937-2005), defense attorney in the O.J. Simpson trial, 120
Cohen, Felix S., lawyer and legal scholar, 72
Cohen, Morris (1880-1947), Russian-born American philosopher, 5, 9
Cohn, Roy M. (1927-1986), American lawyer , 44
Colden, Cadwallader (1688-1776), British-American politician, 76
Coleridge, Samuel Taylor (1772-1834), English poet, 24
Colton, Charles C. (1780-1832), English clergyman and writer, 157
Compton, Lynn, Los Angeles Chief Deputy District Attorney, 151
Condo, Joe, 128
Conine, Ernest (b. 1925), American journalist, 107
Cook, Peter (1937-1995), British writer and entertainer, 46
Cooney, Linda, 140
Cooper, Charles J., American lawyer, 87
Cooper, James Fenimore (1789-1851), American writer, 1, 51
Corboy, Philip (b. 1924), American lawyer, 15, 53
Corcoran, Barbara (b. 1911), American writer, 89
Countryman, Vernon (1903-1978), professor, Harvard University, 25
Cox, Archibald (1912-2004), Watergate prosecutor, 85
Cozzens, James Gould (1903-1978), American writer, 70
Cressey, Donald R. (1919-1987), American writer, 31
Crier, Catherine, American judge, 158
Crosby, Norm (b. 1927), American comedian, 54
Cross, Amanda (b. 1926), American literary scholar and writer, 32
Cuomo, Mario (b. 1932), American politician, 64
Curtin, John J., Jr. (b. 1933), American lawyer, 16
Curtis, Charles P. (1860-1948), American lawyer, 71

D

Darden, Christopher (b. 1956), prosecutor in the O.J. Simpson criminal trial, 120
Darling, C. J., 19th-century English judge, 11
Darrow, Clarence (1857-1938), American lawyer and writer, 5, 16, 52, 90
Dauten, Dale, American newspaper columnist, 107
Davis, Angela Yvonne (b. 1944), American civil rights activist and educator, 101
Davis, Dorothy Salisbury (b. 1916), American writer, 146
Defoe, Daniel (1660-1731), English writer, 7, 90, 93

Dershowitz, Alan (b. 1938), American lawyer and Harvard law professor, 33, 42, 76, 107, 114, 126, 151

Dickens, Charles (1812-1870), English writer, 20, 31

Diderot, Denis (1713-1784), French encyclopedist, 84

Dillwyn, Lewis W. (1788-1855), English naturalist, 108

Disraeli, Benjamin (1804-1881), British prime minister, 11, 90

Docquier, L., French aphorist, 17

Douglas, William O. (1898-1980), Supreme Court Justice, 1, 46, 86

Dudley, John, 18th-century American judge, 95

Dunne, Finley Peter (1867-1936), American humorist, 90, 151

Dworkin, Ronald D. (b. 1931), law professor, New York University, 9

E

Ebert, Roger (b. 1942), American film critic, 128

Einstein, Albert (1879-1955), German-born American physicist, 4

Emerson, Ralph Waldo (1803-1882), American writer and poet, 41, 84, 147

Epictetus (342-270 B.C.), Greek philosopher, 10

Erdmann, Martin, American lawyer, 41

Ervin, Samuel, Jr. (1896-1985), United States senator, 43, 76

Evarts, William (1818-1901), American lawyer, 101

F

Ficaro, Mike (b. 1947), American lawyer, 139

Follette, Suzanne La (1893-1983), American politician and feminist, 3

Ford, Gerald R. (1913-2006), 38th President of the United States, 76

Ford, Malcolm, 17

Foreman, Percy (1902-1988), American lawyer, 161

Fortas, Abe (1910-1982), Supreme Court Justice, 44

France, Anatole (1844-1924), French writer, 3

Francis, Henry Waldorf, 109

Frank, Jerome, American judge, 1

Frankfurter, Felix (1882-1965), Supreme Court Justice, 146, 164

Franklin, Benjamin (1706-1790), American statesman and philosopher, 9, 21

Freund, James C. (b. 1934), American lawyer, 161

Frost, David (b. 1939), British television journalist, 146

Frost, Robert (1874-1963), American poet, 52

Fuchsberg, Jacob D. (b. 1913), President, American Trial Lawyers Association, 52

Fuller, Thomas (1608-1661), English writer, 8, 24, 161

G

Gaddis, William (1922-1998), American writer, 94

Galane, Morton (b. 1926), American lawyer, 141

Galsworthy, John (1967-1933), English writer and dramatist, 6

Garcetti, Gil (b. 1941), Los Angeles District Attorney, 120

Gardner, John W. (1912-2002), U.S. Secretary of Health, Education and Welfare, 3

Garner, Bryan A., Editor-in-Chief, Black's Law Dictionary, 142

Garrison, William Lloyd (1805-1879), American abolitionist, 103

Gasset, José Ortega y (1883-1955), Spanish philosopher, 3

Gates, Bill (b. 1955), Chairman of Microsoft, 115

Gerber, Ann, American journalist, 70

Gibbon, Edward (1737-1794), English historian, 8

Gilbert, William S. (1836-1911), English poet and writer, 6

Gilmore, Grant (1910-1982), legal scholar, 157

Giraudoux, Jean (1882-1944), French playwright, 80

Gladstone, William E. (1809-1898), British statesman, 101

Goethe, Johann Wolfgang von (1749-1832), German poet and dramatist, 10

Goldsmith, Oliver (1728-1774), English writer, 21, 148

Goldwater, Barry (1909-1998), American statesman, 96

Goldwyn, Samuel (1882-1974), film producer, 129

Good, Ned (b. 1928), American lawyer, 141

Gore, Albert, Jr. (b. 1948), 45th Vice President of the United States, 161

Gorky, Maxim (1868-1936), Russian writer, 158

Gossett, William T. (b. 1904), President, American Bar Association, 156

Grace, Nancy, American lawyer, 22

Graham, Fred (b. 1931), American lawyer and journalist, 152

Grant, Ulysses S. (1822-1885), 18th President of the United States, 9

Greebler, Arthur (b. 1956), American lawyer, 29

Greene, Lord Wilfrid Arthur (1883-1952), English judge, 29

Greer, Todd, law student, University of Arkansas, 126

Grossman, Moses Henry (1873-1942), American judge, 109

H

Hand, Learned (1872-1961), U.S. Court of Appeals judge, 90, 134

Haneker, James Gibbons, 142

Harington, Sir John (1561-1612), English writer and translator, 157

Harris, Sydney J. (1917-1986), British-American writer, 71

Harrison, Benjamin (1833-1901), 23rd President of the United States, 155

Harrison II, Moses W. (b. 1932), Illinois Supreme Court Justice, 152

Hart, Frances Noyes (1890-1943), 114
Hathaway, George (1852-1903), American writer, 18
Hays, Arthur (1881-1954), American lawyer, 21
Hellman, Lillian (1905-1984), American dramatist, 102
Hertz, Joseph H. (1872-1946), British-born Hungarian rabbi, 94
Hickerson, Harold, American writer, 42
Higgins, Ladner V., 57
Hinkson, Katherine T. (1861-1931), Irish poet and writer, 24
Hodel, Mathew A. (b. 1955), American lawyer, 126, 162
Holmes, Oliver Wendell, Jr. (1809-1894), Supreme Court Justice, 45, 113,
    157, 158
Holyday, Barten, 17th-century English translator, 133
Hooker, Richard (1554-1600), English theologian, 6
Hooks, Benjamin (b. 1925), Chairman, National Association of Colored
    People, 63
Hoover, J. Edgar (1895-1972), Director, FBI, 90
Horace (65-8 B.C.), Roman poet and satirist, 45, 89
Horsley, Samuel (1733-1806), English bishop, 83
Houser, Dick, 33
Hubbard, Elbert (1856-1915), American writer and editor, 20, 53, 150
Hughes, Charles Evans (1862-1948), Supreme Court Justice, 147
Humphrey, Hubert (1911-1978), 38th Vice President of the United States, 85
Hunt, Lamar (1932-2006), owner, Kansas City Chiefs football team, 19

I

Ingersoll, Robert G. (1844-1915), American lawyer, 91
Ingram, Thomas Lewis, 133
Irving, Clifford, American lawyer, 141
Irving, Washington (1783-1859), American writer, 22
Israels, Richard (b. 1946), Canadian lawyer, 75, 91, 134
Ito, Lance (b. 1950), judge in the O.J. Simpson trial, 46

J

Jackson, Jesse (b. 1941), American clergyman and civil rights activist, 92
Jackson, Robert H. (1892-1954), Supreme Court Justice, 80, 163
Jaworski, Leon (1905-1982), special prosecutor for the Watergate trials, 2
Jefferson, Thomas (1743-1826), 3rd President of the United States, 9, 42, 45, 75
Jenkins, John A., journalist and legal writer, 150
Johnson, Phillip E. (b. 1940), law professor, University of California, 71
Johnston, Neal, Chief of Staff, New York City Council, 37
Justinian I (483-565), Emperor of Byzantine, 94

K

Kafka, Franz (1883-1924), Czechoslovakian novelist, 23

Kallen, Lucille (1932-1999), television comedy writer, 15

Katzenbach, John (b. 1950), American journalist

Kaufman, Irving R. (1910-1992), U.S. Court of Appeals judge, 16, 42, 127, 146

Keats, John (1795-1821), English poet, 19

Keeva, Steven, American journalist, 163

Kellett, Christine (b. 1942), law professor, Dickinson School of Law, 63

Kennedy, Florynce Rae (1916-2000), American lawyer and civil rights activist, 25, 150

Kennedy, John F. (1917-1963), 35th President of the United States, 93

Kennedy, Robert F. (1925-1968), U.S. Attorney General, 91, 102, 164

Kimble, Joseph, professor, Thomas M. Cooley Law School, 130

King, Dr. Martin Luther, Jr. (1929-1968), American clergyman and civil rights leader, 5, 83, 85, 102

Kinsley, Michael (b. 1951), American journalist, 147

Kissinger, Henry (b. 1923), National Security Advisor and Secretary of State, 86

Klieman, Rikki, American lawyer, 33, 54

Kumble, Steven J. (b. 1933), American lawyer, 29

L

Landor, Walter Savage (1775-1864), English writer, 9

Landsman, Stephan (b. 1946), law professor, Marshall College, 145

Lec, Stanislaw (1909-1966), Czech writer, 89

Lee, Harper (b. 1926), American writer, 102

Lenin, Nikolai (1870-1924), Russian revolutionary leader, 43

Lennon, John (1940-1980), 4

Leno, Jay (b. 1950), American comedian, 63

Lessing, Doris (b. 1919), British writer, 162

Liddy, G. Gordon (b. 1930), convicted Nixon presidential aide, 146

Liebowitz, Alan, law firm auditor, 134

Lillie, Charisse R. (b. 1952), Chair of the American Bar Association Commission for Opportunities for Minorities in the Profession, 23

Liman, Arthur (1932-1997), American lawyer, 141

Lincoln, Abraham (1809-1865), 16th President of the United States, 108, 110, 162, 164

Linowitz, Sol M. (b. 1913), American lawyer, 161

Locke, John (1632-1704), English philosopher, 3

Louis XII (1462-1515), King of France, 21

Lycophron, 3rd-century B.C. Greek poet and scholar, 3

M

Machiavelli, Niccolo (1649-1527), Italian statesman and political philosopher, 43

MacKinnon, Catharine (b. 1946), American law professor, feminist and writer, 8

Macklin, Charles (1697-1797), Irish actor and dramatist, 6

MacLeish, Archibald (1892-1947), American poet, 128

Manausa, Danny (b. 1969), American lawyer, 33

Marcuse, Herbert (1898-1979), German-American philosopher, 6

Mark, Robert (b. 1917), British police commissioner, 114

Marshall, John (1755-1835), Supreme Court Justice, 43

Masterson, Bert, 11

Mayer, Milton (b. 1908), American journalist, 76

McGeorge, John, Australian psychiatrist, 32, 52

McHugh, William F., law professor, Florida State University, 164

McLaughlin, Mignon, American writer, 32

Mellinkoff, David (1914-2000), law professor, UCLA, 126

Mellor, David (b. 1949), 17

Melville, Herman (1819-1891), American writer, 85

Mencken, H. L. (1880-1956), American journalist, 43, 52, 192, 113

Middleton, Thomas (1570-1627), English dramatist, 93

Millay, Edna St. Vincent (1892-1950), American poet, 17

Miller, Edward A. (b. 1931), Florida judge, 149

Miller, Henry G. (b. 1931), former President, New York State Bar Association, 145

Miller, Samuel F. (1816-1890), American judge, 83

Minow, Newton (b. 1926), FCC chairman and lawyer, 53, 146

Montaigne, Michel de (1533-1592), French writer, 86, 155

Montesquieu, Charles Louis de (1689-1755), French lawyer and political philosopher, 3, 155

Moone, Hoyt, American lawyer, 37

Moore, Portia (b. 1955), American lawyer, 57

Morgan, J. P. (1837-1913), American financier, 32

Morgenthau, Robert (b. 1919), New York City District Attorney, 53

Morphonios, Ellen (1929-2002), American judge, 91

Morris, Robert J., American lawyer, 45

Morrison, Peter, American lawyer, 18

Mortimer, John (1923-2009), English lawyer and writer, 53, 164

Myerson, Abraham (1881-1948), Russian-American neuropsychiatrist, 83

N

Naisbitt, John (b. 1929), American writer, 127
Napoleon I (1769-1821), Emperor of France, 6, 91
Nix, Robert N. C., Jr. (1928-2003), United States Congressman, 79
Nixon, Richard (1913-1994), 37th President of the United States, 86
Nizer, Louis (1902-1994), American lawyer, 31, 139, 162
Nolan, John T., 30
Norris, George W. (1861-1944), United States Senator, 64
North, Oliver (b. 1943), Marine Lt. Colonel, 33

O

O'Connor, Sandra Day (b. 1930), Supreme Court Justice, 125, 163
O'Neil, Paul (1909-1988), American writer and journalist, 18, 140
Olson, Walter K. (b. 1954), Senior fellow, Manhattan Institute, 127
Osborn, John Jay, Jr. (b. 1945), American writer, 37
Otway, Thomas (1652-1685), English dramatist, 93
Ouida (1839-1908), Scottish writer, 158
Ovid (43 B.C.-17 A.D.), Roman poet, 10

P

Packard, Edward B., Jr., American lawyer, 79
Paine, Thomas (1737-1819), British-born American political philosopher and
    writer, 75
Palmer, Harry (b. 1939), American lawyer, 25
Pankhurst, Emmeline (1858-1928), English suffragist, 92
Papantonio, Mike (b. 1953), American lawyer, 128
Pavalon, Eugene (b. 1933), American lawyer and president, American Trial
    Lawyers Association, 115
Perry, Robert, American lawyer, 58
Phillips, Wendell (1811-1884), American orator and reformer, 84
Plato (427-347 B.C.), Greek philosopher, 2
Pollock, Frederick (1845-1937), English judge, 108
Polsby, Daniel, law professor, Northwestern University, 54
Pomerantz, Hart, American lawyer, 79
Pound, Roscoe (1870-1964), Dean Emeritus, Harvard Law School, 7, 157
Powell, Adam Clayton , Jr. (1908-1972), American clergyman and United
    States Congressman, 86
Powell, Lewis F., Jr. (1907-1998), Supreme Court Justice, 64, 65
Powell, Thomas Reed (1880-1955), professor, Harvard University, 21
Prosser, William L., legal scholar, 23

Q

Quayle, J. Danforth (b. 1947), 44th Vice President of the United States, 108, 147
Quinn, Jane Bryant (b. 1939), American journalist, 15, 148

R

Reagan, Ronald W. (1911-2004), 40th President of the United States, 155
Rehnquist, William H. (1924-2005), Supreme Court Justice, 41, 155
Ricker, Darlene (b. 1954), American lawyer and legal journalist, 41, 139
Robbins, Tom (b. 1936), American writer, 30
Rochefoucauld, François de la (1613-1680), French writer, 95
Rockefeller, John D., Jr. (1874-1960), American oil magnate and philanthropist, 75
Rodell, Fred (1907-1980), law professor, Yale University, 2, 127
Rogers, Will (1879-1935), American humorist, 23, 30, 71, 129
Roland, Jeanne-Marie (1754-1793), French revolutionary, 102
Roosevelt, Theodore (1858-1919), 26th President of the United States, 9, 185
Root, Elihu (1845-1937), American lawyer and statesman, 30
Rosten, Leo (1908-1997), Polish-American writer, 31
Rothman, David, American lawyer, 152
Rousseau, Jean Jacques (1712-1778), French philosopher and writer, 4
Rubin, Asher (b. 1936), California Deputy Attorney General, 109
Rubin, Ellis (1925-2006), American lawyer, 15
Rymer, Pamela Ann (b. 1941), Los Angeles Federal judge, 70, 126

S

Sandburg, Carl (1878-1967), American writer, 20
Sanger, Margaret (1883-1966), American political activist, 149
Sawyer, Diane (b. 1945), American television journalist, 134
Scalia, Antonin (b. 1936), Supreme Court Justice, 6
Scarman, Lord Leslie (1933-2004), English lawyer, 155
Schulder, Diane B. (b. 1937), American lawyer and educator, 149
Schwartz, Michael Alan (b. 1948), American journalist, 71
Scott, Sir Walter (1771-1832), Scottish poet and writer, 20, 24
Seebach, Linda, American journalist, 108
Seneca (4 B.C.-65 A.D.), Roman statesman and philosopher, 43
Shapiro, Irving S. (1916-2001), American industrialist, 109
Shapiro, Robert (b. 1942), defense attorney in the O. J. Simpson trial, 140
Shays, Ruth, 147, 155
Shea, Edward F., Jr. (b. 1925), American lawyer, 126
Sherman, Charles E., American lawyer, 142

Sherman, Norm, American lawyer, 80

Singer, Alyson, American lawyer, 7

Smiles, Samuel (1812-1904), English writer, 10

Smith, Elliott Dunlap (1891-1976), American writer, 127

Smith, Sydney (1771-1845), English writer, 10, 155

Socrates, 4th-century B.C. Greek philosopher, 97

Solzhenitsyn, Alexander (1918-2008), Russian writer, 145, 152

Sophocles (496-406 B.C.), Greek dramatist, 69

Soucy, Dave (b. 1955), American lawyer, 24

Spence, Gerry (b. 1929), American lawyer, 79, 140

Spencer, Herbert (1820-1903), English philosopher, 54

Spicer, David (b. 1948), American lawyer, 93

Stanton, Elizabeth Cady (1815-1902), American suffragist, 84

Starr, Kenneth (b. 1946), Special Prosecutor, 86

Stein, Sol, American businessman and writer, 20

Steinem, Gloria (b. 1934), American writer and feminist, 155

Stemple, Jeff, law professor, Florida State University, 134

Sterling, John (1844-1918), American lawyer, 30

Stevenson, Adlai E. (1900-1965), American lawyer and diplomat, 37, 57, 127

Stevenson, Melford (1902-1987), British judge, 114

Stewart, E. Ralph, 145

Stewart, Potter (1915-1985), Supreme Court Justice, 46, 92

Stracher, Cameron, American lawyer, 110

Stryker, Lloyd Paul (b. 1955), American lawyer, 114

Surtees, Robert Smith (1806-1864), English novelist, 22

Sykes, Charles, American author, 33

Syrus, Publilius, 1st-century B.C. Roman writer, 43, 45, 87

Szasz, Thomas, professor, Syracuse University, 87

T

Tacitus (c. 56-120), Roman historian, 44

Taft, William Howard (1857-1930), 27th President of the United States, 113

Theognis, 6th-century B.C. Greek poet, 93

Thomas, H. James (b. 1960), American lawyer, 25

Thompson, James R. (b. 1936), Illinois Governor, 152

Thoreau, Henry David (1817-1872), American writer, 8, 103

Tocqueville, Alexis de (1805-1859), French statesman and writer, 53, 150

Tolstoy, Leo (1828-1910), Russian philosopher and author, 77

Townsend, Robert (1920-1998), American businessman, 19

Train, Arthur (1875-1945), American lawyer and writer, 23

Traver, Robert (1903-1993), American writer and judge, 38

Trillin, Calvin, American writer, 80

Trollope, Anthony (1815-1882), English writer, 134
Truman, Harry S. (1884-1972), 33rd President of the United States, 65
Turow, Scott (b. 1949), American lawyer and novelist, 15
Twain, Mark (1835-1910), American writer and humorist, 19, 52, 151
Tweed, Harrison (1885-1969), American lawyer, 19

U

Udall, Morris K. (1922-1998), United States Congressman, 65

V

Veeck, Bill, owner, Chicago White Sox, 147
Vidal, Gore (b. 1925), American writer, 109
Voltaire (1694-1778), French writer, 10, 110, 147

W

Wapner, Joseph A. (b. 1919), American judge, 42, 125, 145
Warren, Earl (189-1974), Supreme Court Justice, 69
Wartowski, Thomas A. (b. 1947), American lawyer, 2, 87
Washington, George (1732-1799), 1st President of the United States, 87, 96
Waters, John (b. 1946), American filmmaker, 115
Webster, Daniel (1782-1852), American statesman, orator and lawyer, 4, 16, 69, 140, 163
Weinberger, Caspar W. (1917-2006), publisher, 109
Weinkrantz, Herman, American judge, 91
Wells, Ida B. (1862-1931), American journalist, 102
Whalen, Grover A. (1886-1962), New York City police commissioner, 84
Whichcote, Benjamin (1609-1683), English philosophical theologian, 45
White, Daniel R. (b. 1953), American writer, 80
Whitman, Walt (119-1892), American poet, 92
Wilde, Oscar (1854-1900), Irish writer, 141
Willis, Garry, Northwestern University history professor, 77
Wilson, Earl, American journalist, 11
Wilson, Frank W. (1917-1990), American judge, 95
Wilson, Woodrow (1856-1924), 28th President of the United States, 92, 140
Wycherley, William (1640-1716), English writer, 24
Wydick, Richard, American lawyer, 33

Y

Yevtushenko, Yevgeny (b. 1933), Russian poet, 92
Younger, Evelle J., American lawyer, 148
Yutang, Lin, Chinese writer, 97
Yuter, S. C., American journalist and writer, 7

Z

Zagrans, Eric (b. 1953), American lawyer, 57
Zerman, Melvyn B. (b. 1930), American writer, 54
Zobel, Hiller B. (b. 1932), American judge, 120
Zuckerman, Mortimer (b. 1937), American editor and publisher, 2

About Carbolic Smoke Ball Co.

The Carbolic Smoke Ball Co. is named after the famous law case of 1892, *Carlill v. Carbolic Smoke Ball Co.*, which clarified the important principle of offer and consideration in contract law.

Our namesake went into liquidation in 1893, shortly after the Court of Appeal decided that the company's offer of £100 to anyone who used its patented smoke ball yet contracted influenza was an offer that had to be honoured and not a 'mere puff'. For the last 17 years, we have avoided that fate, selling a wide variety of law-themed stationery and gifts to solicitors and barristers worldwide. Our website is at:

www.carbolicsmokeball.com

There you will find:

- The best law cartoons from the *Punch* archives, available framed, for your office wall.
- A wide selection of classic law pictures, including Vanity Fair, law buildings, the Inns of Court etc.
- Cufflinks and jewellery bearing legal motifs.
- Ties, t-shirts and sweatshirts with legal slogans.
- Lawyer's Christmas and greeting cards.
- Coffee mugs, coasters and paperweights.
- Gavels, lecterns, wig boxes, and other accessories.
- Hundred of other law-themed products . . .

Carbolic Smoke Ball Co. – Contact Details

If you would like a copy of the latest Carbolic Smoke Ball Co. catalogue, or want to get in touch with us for any other reason, please contact us by one of these means:

Phone: +44 1252 795951

Fax: +44 1252 790777

Email: enquiries@carbolicsmokeball.com

Post: Carbolic Smoke Ball Co.
          Silverbeck
          Jumps Road
          Churt
          Farnham
          Surrey
          GU10 2HL
          United Kingdom